A Journey through
ANCIENT EGYPT

BROCKHAMPTON PRESS

First published in Great Britain in 1998 by
BROCKHAMPTON PRESS
20 Bloomsbury Street, London WC1B 3QA
a member of the Hodder Headline Group

ISBN 1-86019-832-5

Conceived and designed by Savitri Books Ltd

The first impression of Karnak is that of a palace of giants.

Gustave Flaubert, *Travel Notes* (1850)

Endpapers. This scene belongs to the Book of the Dead, *a collection of paintings, accompanied by magical texts, executed on papyrus and placed inside a tomb to facilitate the passage of the soul through the Underworld. The couple shown on the left, at the bottom of the picture, awaits judgement as the husband's heart is weighed against an ostrich feather representing Maat, the goddess of truth, justice and cosmic order. Anubis, the jackal-headed god of the dead, checks the accuracy of the procedure. Thoth, the god of scribes and of learning, represented with the head of an ibis, is getting ready to inscribe the result. Behind him stands Ammit, the hybrid monster whose role was to gobble up any heart weighed down by sin.*

INTRODUCTION

Egypt has become a highly popular travel and holiday destination – hardly surprising in view of the richness of its cultural heritage. The fascination is not a recent one, as will be seen from the reactions of writers through the ages to the land and the strange attraction it exerts. From Herodotus to Flaubert and on to modern-day travel writers such as Eric Newby, all recorded their awe at the buildings and the civilisation which brought them into being – as well as their enjoyment, even if at times tinged with irritation, of the colourful life and the warmth of the people they encountered on their travels.

The map opposite shows the river Nile as it makes its way through the land of Egypt. The Nile is the longest river in the world, stretching for a distance of 4,163 miles. The Great – Egyptian – Nile is formed by the merging of the White Nile, which rises in the Rwenzori mountain range in Zaire, and the Blue Nile, which rises in the high plateaux of Ethiopia. It flows into the Mediterranean via a vast delta system. Alluvium deposited over the centuries has helped to create an extremely fertile strip (up to 12½ miles wide), which has given rise to a rich and diversified agriculture.

Ancient Egypt relied on yearly floods for its prosperity. Today, the introduction of irrigation which followed the construction of the Aswan High Dam ensures the prosperity of this 'linear oasis' while controlling the often disastrous effects of the floods.

In some areas, the fertile cultivated strip on either side of the river is sufficiently narrow to enable the traveller to observe the clear demarcation between the lush greenness of irrigated land and the yellow-brown aridity of the desert beyond. This

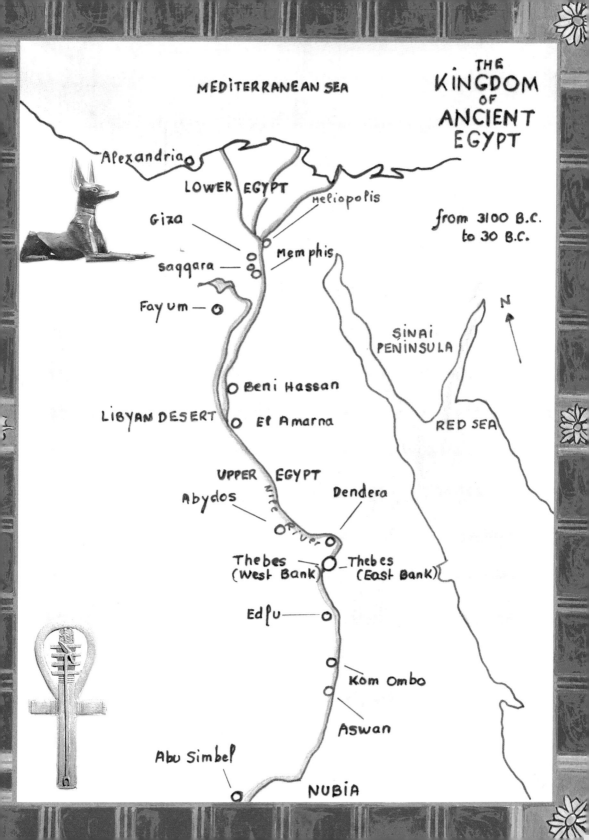

is one of the abiding memories of the journey up or down river, watching the *fellaheen* going about their tasks, the villages shaded by date palms and surrounded by small, unbelievably green fields where rice, corn, sunflowers and cotton grow in abundance. Succulent vegetables and fruits are also produced and have helped to create a varied and tasty cuisine.

The boat deck is also a very good observation point for the rich birdlife which depends on the Nile for its survival. The abundance and variety of the fauna explains the fascination exercised by the animal world on the Ancient Egyptians, a fascination expressed in the complex pantheon of gods and recorded on the wall paintings and the papyrus scrolls found in the tombs. The tradition of painting on papyrus is emulated by modern Egyptian artists, as the illustrations in this book show.

The map also shows the principal sites and buildings of Ancient Egypt which have survived the onslaughts of time.

Ancient Egyptian history is divided into three main periods, called the Old Kingdom (c. 2613–2160 BC), the Middle Kingdom (c. 2040–1750 BC) and the New Kingdom (c. 1550–1086 BC). The region known as Upper Egypt covered the Nile Valley from about the site of modern Cairo as far south as Aswan; its symbol was the lotus flower. Lower Egypt began at the point where the Nile fanned out to create a delta of marshy, fertile land and was represented by the papyrus plant. These symbols appear on a myriad of wall panels and tomb paintings. The traveller beginning a little south of Aswan, at Abu Simbel in the old kingdom of Nubia, and sailing down the Nile towards the delta would pass within a few miles of most of the major sites of Ancient Egypt.

Abu Simbel is the site of the great temple of Ramesses II (1279–1213 BC), one of the most self-aggrandising of all the pharaohs. In the course of his long reign he earned the title 'the

Opposite. *The Egyptian cosmos. Ra is seen at the bottom of the picture, rolling the sun across the sky.*

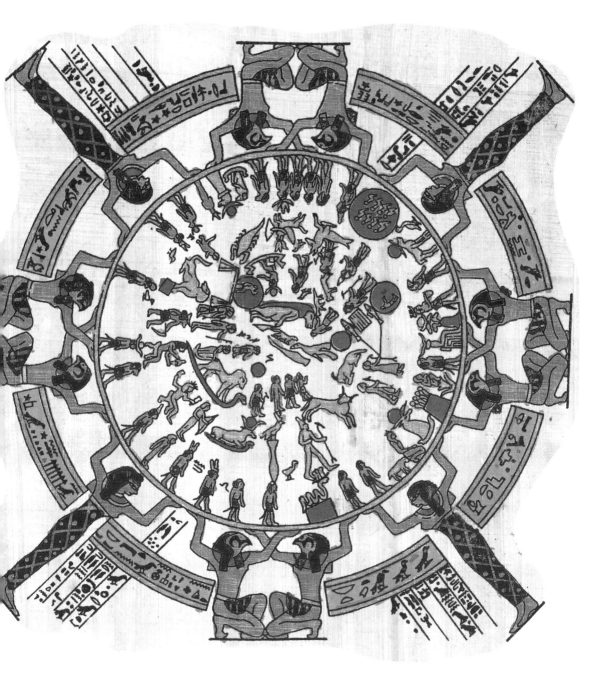

Great': in addition to being a successful warrior, he built more colossal monuments than any other pharaoh. The temple at Abu Simbel is on a massive scale, carved out of the natural sandstone with four vast figures of Ramesses himself flanking the entrance.

When Gamal Abd el-Nasser decided on the construction of the Aswan High Dam in 1954, entailing the flooding of over 300 miles of the Nile Valley – in other words the whole of Nubia as far as the second cataract – many archaeological sites would have disappeared under water, most notably the enormous temple complex at Abu Simbel. An international rescue programme was launched to undertake a complete survey of sites under threat and to mount a rescue operation for the most important monuments. At Abu Simbel, the entire structure was cut up into enormous blocks, which were numbered and transported 210 feet further up the cliff. They were then reconstructed according to their original position and orientation over a reinforced concrete structure. This mammoth task took three years and a 3000-strong workforce. The temple re-opened officially in September 1968.

Aswan was the site of the temple of Philae, dedicated to Isis. The High Dam and the enormous Lake Nasser flooded the island on which the temple was built. A movable dam was installed to enable the dismantling of the building, which was also rebuilt well above the water level.

The next stop on the boat trip is probably Kom Ombo, which houses a temple dedicated to Sobek, the crocodile god. Crocodiles were common in the Nile; they were worshipped and often mummified after death. Next comes Edfu, the site of a temple erected to Horus, the falcon-god who was the son of Osiris, god of the afterlife.

Beyond Aswan the visitor comes to Thebes, capital of the New Kingdom. Here are to be found the great temples of Luxor and Karnak, another temple of Ramesses the Great, the temple of Queen Hatshepsut and the Valley of Kings, best known for the treasure-laden tomb of the young pharaoh Tutankhamen. The approach to Karnak is via the 2-mile long Avenue of the Sphinxes, which was once lined with sphinxes, each bearing a statue of Ramesses between her paws.

Next ports of call are Abydos, centre of the cult of Osiris, and Dendera, site of the temple of Hathor, goddess of love. Then the Nile threads its way to El Amarna, the site of the doomed capital Akhenaten, built in the fourteenth century BC by the pharaoh of the same name. Here he introduced a new art style and the later much-reviled cult of the sun disk, the Aten, as the dominant aspect of Egyptian religion. Akhenaten was married to Queen Nefertiti, whose painted but unfinished limestone bust, found near El Amarna at the beginning of this century, is considered the epitome of the new, more realistic art form favoured by Akhenaten. The adherents of the old religion exacted their revenge on Akhenaten by destroying his capital after his death. The city was inhabited for a mere eleven years.

Bèni Hassan is the site of tombs carved out of rock. They contained paintings which depict scenes of everyday life. Fayum houses a Roman cemetery in which were found several Egyptian-style monuments with realistic Roman-style portraits over their faces.

Memphis was the capital of the Old Kingdom – the city has disappeared, together with the temple dedicated to Ptah, god of craftsmen. Close by present-day Cairo stands the great Pyramid of Khufu or Cheops at Giza, with the smaller ones of Khafre and Menkaura. Together with the statue of the Sphinx, they bear witness to the monumental building skills of the Old Kingdom.

The city of Alexandria was founded by Alexander the Great and was the site of the Pharos lighthouse, one of the wonders of the ancient world, demolished in the thirteenth century AD.

For many centuries scholars and travellers alike have been awestruck by the sheer scale of the Egyptian monuments.

I went last night to look at Karnac by moonlight. The giant columns were overpowering. I never saw anything so solemn.

Lady Duff Gordon, *Letters from Egypt* (1862-69)

We had scarcely gone a quarter of a league when we saw the summit of the two great pyramids. The appearance of these ancient monuments that have survived the destruction of nations, the fall of empires, the ravages of time, inspires a kind of reverence. The soul glances over the centuries that have flowed past their unshakeable bulk and experiences an involuntary shudder of awe. Let us salute these remains of the Seven Wonders of the World! And pay tribute to those who raised them!

Jacques Savary, *Letters Written from Egypt* (1779)

Though its proportions are colossal, [the Sphinx's] contours are as delicate as correct. The expression of the head is soft, gracious, and tranquil. The character is African, but the mouth, the lips of which are thick, has a sweetness in its drawing and an elegance in its execution which are truly admirable: it is absolutely flesh and life.

Dominique Vivant Denon,
Travels in Upper and Lower Egypt (1803)

About Egypt itself I shall have a great deal more to relate because of the number of remarkable things which the country contains, and because of the fact that more monuments which beggar description are to be found there than anywhere else in the world. That is reason enough for my dwelling on it at greater length. Not only is the Egyptian climate peculiar to that country, and the Nile different in its behaviour from other rivers elsewhere, but the Egyptians themselves in their manners and customs seem to have reversed the ordinary practices of mankind. For instance, women attend market and are employed in trade, while men stay at home and do the weaving. In weaving the normal way is to work the threads of the weft upwards, but the Egyptians work them downwards. Men in Egypt carry loads on their heads, women on their shoulders; women pass water standing up, men sitting down. To ease themselves they go indoors, but eat outside in the streets, on the theory that what is unseemly but necessary should be done in private, and what is not unseemly should be done openly. No woman holds priestly office, either in the service of goddess or god; only men are priests in both cases. Sons are under no compulsion to support their parents if they do not wish to do so, but daughters must, whether they wish it or not. Elsewhere priests grow their hair long; in Egypt they shave their heads. In other nations the relatives of the deceased in time of mourning cut their hair, but the Egyptians, who shave at all other times, mark a death by letting the hair grow both on head and chin. They live with their animals – unlike the rest of the world, who live apart from them. Other men live on wheat and barley, but any Egyptian who does so is blamed for it, their bread being made from spelt, or *Xea* as some call it. Dough they knead with their feet, but clay with their hands – and even handle dung. They practise circumcision, while men of other nations – except those who

16

The phoenix travelling with the barque of the sun god. A clump of papyrus symbolises Lower Egypt.

have learnt from Egypt – leave their private parts as nature made them. Men in Egypt have two garments each, women only one. The ordinary practice at sea is to make sheets fast to ring-bolts fitted outboard; the Egyptians fit them inboard. In writing or calculating, instead of going, like the Greeks, from left to right, the Egyptians go from right to left – and obstinately maintain that theirs is the dexterous method, ours being left-handed and awkward. They have two sorts of writing, the sacred and the common. They are religious to excess, beyond any other nation in the world, and here are some of the customs which illustrate the fact: they drink from brazen cups which they scour every day – everyone, without exception. They wear linen clothes which they make a special point of continually washing. They circumcise themselves for cleanliness' sake, preferring to be clean rather than comely.

Herodotus, *History* (5th century BC)

Now stretching out before us is an immense plain, very green, with squares of black soil which are the fields most recently ploughed, the last from which the flood withdrew: they stand out like India ink on the solid green. I think of the invocation to Isis: 'Hail, hail, black soil of Egypt!'

Gustave Flaubert, *Travel Notes* (1949)

The alien and mysterious Nile, that gigantic serpent that winds so fabulously, so ungraspably, back through history.

Rose Macaulay, *Pleasures of Ruins* (1953)

Unable to make a map of the country, I took a bird's-eye view of the entrance of the Nile into Egypt, and views of this river, rolling its water among the sharp rocks of granite which seem to have marked the limits of burning Ethiopia and of a country more happy and more temperate.

Dominique Vivant Denon,
Travels in Upper and Lower Egypt (1803)

Thus far we have come quite safely & with great pleasure. I wrote to you from Cairo – on the 12th – just before we were going to start, & I told you that I had already tried my camel, which conveyance both Cross & myself found admirably easy & pleasant. I cannot tell why people write such nonsense about the East as they do: regarding the camel, you have only to sit quite still when it rises, & hold fast by the saddle – & you are lifted up on the long necked monster – & away you go *just as if on a rocking chair*. – But the great beauty of the camelriding is the size of the sort of table you sit on – made up of pillows, & coats, & carpets, & saddlebags: – we sit crosslegged – or opposite each other, or we turn round – just as we please, & we lunch or read as quietly as if we were in a room. Nothing can be more charming. As for the camels themselves – I cannot say much for them: they *are* quite harmless & quiet, but *seem* the most odious beasts – except when they are moving. The sort of horrible way in which they growl & snarl if you only go 6 feet near them – is quite frightful – & if you did not know them – you would suppose they were going to eat you. They do the same to their own masters the Arabs – & appear to have the most unsociable disposition in the world – even among themselves. I give my camel a bunch of green morning

& evening – but all attempts at making friends are useless: When I put the vegetable within a yard of him, he yells & grunts as if I were killing him – & after he has taken & eaten it he does just the same. – They all seem to say – 'Oh! bother you! can't you let me alone!' – & are certainly uninteresting quadrupeds as to their social qualities. – Their pace is *just* 3 miles an hour – like clockwork: If you try to make them go faster – they growl: if you stop them or try to go slower, they growl also. – They will have their own way. It is a wonderful thing to see the long long strings of these strange creatures crossing the desert – silently striding along – laden with bales of goods. One & all have the same expression – 'I am going from Suez to Cairo to please you – but don't speak to me or come near me: – I shall go on very well if you let me alone – but if you only look at me I'll growl –' – At night, when our tent is pitched, all the camels stride away – just where they please – looking for little thorny shrubs they feed on – till quite out of sight: but after sunset – when the Arabs call them, they all appear in 2s and threes – & are soon round the tent fires – where they are all tethered & have a lot of beans given them – & there they stay till morning. Most of them make a nasty noise as if they were sick all night long. – At sunrise, they are disturbed to be loaded, & then the groans & grumblings begin & go on till we are fairly off.

Edward Lear (1812–88), *Letter to his Wife*

Our first ride in the Desert, was full of wonder and delight. It was only about three miles: but it might have been thirty for the amount of novelty in it. Our thick umbrellas, covered with brown holland, were a necessary protection against the heat, which would have been almost intolerable, but for the cool north wind. – I believed before that I had

imagined the Desert: but now I felt that nobody could. No one could conceive the confusion of piled and scattered rocks, which, even in a ride of three miles, deprives a stranger of all sense of direction, except by the heavens. These narrow passes among black rocks, all suffocation and glare, without shade or relief, are the very home of despair. The oppression of the sense of sight disturbs the brain, so that the will of the unhappy wanderer cannot keep his nerves in order... The presence of dragon-flies in the Desert surprised me; – not only here, but in places afterwards – where there appeared to be no water within a great distance. To those who have been wont to watch the coming forth of the dragon-fly from its sheath on the rush on the margin of a pool, and flitting about the mountain watercourse, or in the moist meadows at home, it is strange to see them by dozens glittering in the sunshine of the Desert, where there appears to be nothing for them to alight on: – nothing that would not shrivel them up, if they rested for a moment from the wing. The hard dry locust seemed more in its place, and the innumerable beetles, which everywhere left a net-work of delicate tracks on the light sand. Distant figures are striking in the desert, in the extreme clearness of light and shade. Shadows strike upon the sense here as bright lights do elsewhere. It seems to me that I remember every figure I ever saw in the Desert; – every veiled woman tending her goats, or carrying her water-jar on her head; – every man in blue skirting the hillocks; every man in brown guiding his ass or his camel through the sandy defiles of the black rocks, or on a slope by moonlight, when he casts a long shadow. Every moving thing has a new value to the eye in such a region.

Harriet Martineau, *Eastern Life, Present and Past* (1848)

At length I saw the portico of Hermopolis; and the vast masses of its ruins gave me the first image of the colossal architecture of the Egyptians; on each rock that composed this edifice, there seemed to be engraved, POSTERITY, ETERNITY.

Dominique Vivant Denon,
Travels in Upper and Lower Egypt (1803)

The 'Dromedary' of Egypt and Syria is not the two-humped animal described by that name in books of natural history, but is in fact of the same family as the camel, to which it stands in about the same relation as a racer to a cart-horse. The fleetness and endurance of this creature are extraordinary. It is not usual to force him into a gallop, and I fancy from his make that it would be quite impossible for him to maintain that pace for any length of time, but the animal is on so large a scale, that the jog-trot at which he is generally ridden implies a progress of perhaps ten or twelve miles an hour, and this pace, it is said, he can keep up incessantly without food, or water, or rest for three whole days, and nights.
Of the two dromedaries which I had obtained for this journey, I mounted one myself and put Dthemetri on the other. My plan was, to ride on with Dthemetri to Suez as rapidly as the fleetness of the beasts would allow, and to let Mysseri (who was still weak from the effects of his late illness) come quietly on with the camels, and baggage. The trot of the Dromedary is a pace terribly disagreeable to the rider, until he becomes a little accustomed to it; but after the first half hour I so far schooled myself to this new exercise, that I felt capable of keeping it up (though not without aching limbs) for several hours together. Now,

therefore, I was anxious to dart forward and annihilate at once the whole space that divided me from the Red Sea. Dthemetri, however, could not get on at all; every attempt which he made to trot seemed to threaten the utter dislocation of his whole frame, and indeed I doubt whether any one of Dthemetri's age (nearly forty, I think) and unaccustomed to such exercise could have borne it at all easily; besides, the dromedary which fell to his lot was evidently a very bad one; he every now and then came to a dead stop, and coolly knelt down as though suggesting that the rider had better get off at once, and abandon the attempt as one that was utterly hopeless.

Alexander Kinglake, *Eothen, or Traces of Travel Brought Home from the East* (1844)

THE LAND OF EGYPT

Apart from the delta and the lush mangrove forests adjacent to the Red Sea, the land of Ancient Egypt was overwhelmingly desert – today, 96 per cent of the country receives less than an inch of rain a year. A few well-adapted plants such as acacia bushes dot the landscape, but even they struggle in times of drought. The mangrove swamps teem with life and are a rich and fertile fishing ground, but are too marshy to support large communities of people. The massive dugong or sea cow, whose habit of sitting almost upright in the water gave rise to the legends of mermaids, has vanished from many parts of the world, but can still be found along the Red Sea and must have been common in ancient times. The swamps provide nesting sites for turtles and breeding grounds for such dramatic birds as the osprey and the Western reef heron. But only in the vicinity of the Nile could people live comfortably and grow enough food to feed themselves.

The Nile flooded every year, covering the surrounding land for about four months and, when the waters receded, leaving behind a rich layer of muddy soil into which the people could sow the next season's crops. The fertile black silt, carried by the floodwaters hundreds of miles down river from the sources of the Nile in modern Uganda and Ethiopia, was the basis of Egypt's wealth.

The importance of the Nile as a means of communication can be seen in the diversity of boats that the Ancient Egyptians produced. Boats were used for hunting and fishing, for transporting people and goods – notably the masses of stone used in the pyramids and temples – and as vehicles of war. They even had a ceremonial role. Many of the gods had their own sacred 'barques', and barques were the favoured means of transport for the dead on their way to the afterlife: models of boats have frequently been found in tombs.

Timber was scarce, but aquatic plants were abundant, so the ever-resourceful Egyptians built boats from papyrus stems bound together with ropes made from other plants. The result was a light, buoyant craft ideal for fishing in shallow water. For more substantial vessels precious woods such as cedar and sycamore were used: over 400 tons of granite to form the two obelisks of Queen Hatshepsut at Thebes (one of which is still standing) was brought from Aswan in a huge sycamore boat with a specially reinforced deck.

In contrast to the black lands of the Nile floodplain, the rest of the country was harsh red desert. But although inhospitable to human life, the desert was a rich source of stone and minerals: the granite, sandstone and limestone used to build the great monuments; and the gold, copper and semi-precious stones with which the Egyptians made and decorated ornaments and utensils.

Ancient Egyptian farming methods were remarkably sophisticated: they had the plough as early as 2000 BC, and they harvested their barley and wheat with sickles whose teeth were carved from flint. By the time of the New Kingdom they could draw water from wells with a bucket balanced by a counter-weight. In addition to food, they grew flax, which could be made into linen for clothing and papyrus for writing, and whose oil was used for cooking and in lamps. Every part of the palm tree was used – the wood of the trunk for fuel; the leaves woven into mats, baskets or furniture.

Because the farmlands were flooded for four months of the year, the farmers and farm workers – who made up most of the population – might have been unemployed throughout this period. Instead, they worked for 'the government', perhaps contributing to the enormous workforce which made the construction of the pyramids possible.

Egypt once seen was never forgotten. Travellers have always found themselves haunted with memories of Egypt, and Egyptians abroad yearn to return home. As Mika Waltari wrote in *The Egyptian*:

Anyone who has drunk of the waters of the Nile seeks to return to the Nile, for no other water can slake their thirst. Anyone born in Thebes seeks to return to Thebes, for no other city in the world can compare with Thebes. Anyone born in a street in Thebes seeks to return to that street; in cedarwood palaces they long for a hut built of clay; amidst the scent of myrrh and perfumed unguents, they long for the smell of dried cow-dung burning on the fire and the aroma of fried fish.

At dawn in the morning we were on deck; the character had not altered of the scenery about the river. Vast flat stretches of land were on either side, recovering from the subsiding inundations: near the mud villages, a country ship or two was roosting under the date trees; the landscape everywhere stretching away level and lonely. In the sky to the east was a long streak of greenish light, which widened and rose until it grew to be of an opal colour, then orange, then, behold, the round red disk of the sun rose flaming up above the horizon. All the water blushed as he got up; the deck was all red; the steersman gave his helm to another, and prostrated himself on the deck, and bowed his head eastward, and praised the Maker of the sun:

Below. A man makes obeisance to Osiris, the god of the afterlife, shown carrying a crook, a flair and a was-sceptre. The table in front of the deity is piled high with offerings.

it shone on his white turban as he was kneeling, and gilt up his bronzed face, and sent his blue shadow over the glowing deck. The distances, which had been grey, were now clothed in purple; and the broad stream was illuminated. As the sun rose higher, the morning blush faded away; the sky was cloudless and pale, and the river and the surrounding landscape were dazzlingly clear.

Looking ahead in an hour or two, we saw the Pyramids. Fancy my sensations, dear M—; – two big ones and a little one: There they lay, rosy and solemn in the distance – those old majestical, mystical familiar edifices. Several of us tried to be impressed; but breakfast supervening, a rush was made on the coffee and cold pies, and the sentiment of awe was lost in the scramble for victuals.

William Makepeace Thackeray, *Notes of a Journey from Cornhill to Grand Cairo* (1865)

The situation of Thebes is as beautiful as fancy can conceive it.

Dominique Vivant Denon,
Travels in Upper and Lower Egypt (1803)

The Nile passes through Cairo like a stranger. In all its long journey from the heart of Africa, it has seen nothing like this... The river is like a fellahin newly arrived from the countryside, appalled, hoping to pass through the city unnoticed. Like everything in Egypt, Cairo is the creation of the Nile, but the river and the city seem estranged.

Stanley Stuart, *Old Serpent Nile*

The cartouche of Tutankhamun (1334–1325 BC).

Below. Maat, the goddess of truth, kneels with her protective wings outstretched in front of the goddess Hathor, who holds a sistrum in her left hand. Maat wears the symbolic ostrich feather on her head. Hathor is frequently represented with the head of a cow and is then a symbol of motherly love.

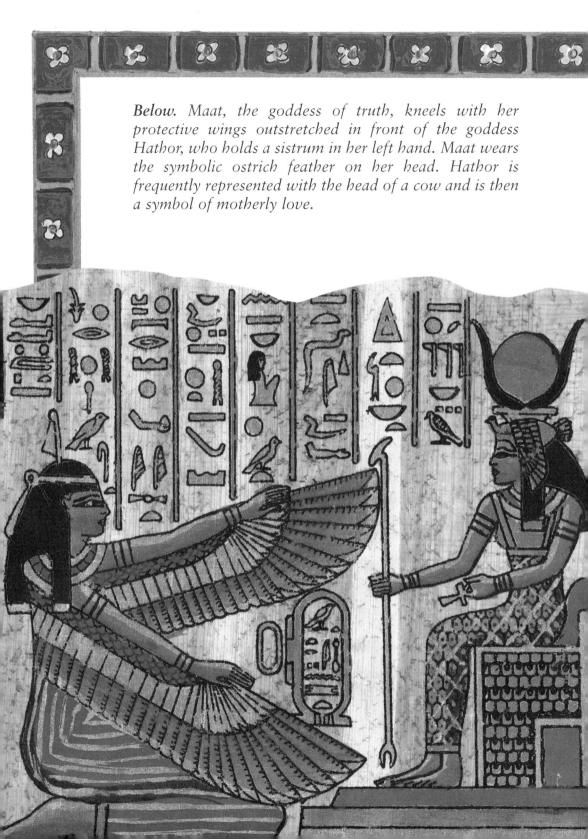

No place can be better than the Egyptian desert for such a trip; good weather for the greater part of the year, wonderful fresh air, excellent transport and freedom to go exploring and to pitch the tent where fancy dictates. Then there is the much talked of 'fascination and mystery of the desert'. – It is there, sure enough, no doubt about it: the sunrises and sunsets, the outgoing of the morning and the evening, the nights of pearly moonlight or clear, starry darkness, the solitude, the great silence and the wide spaces. The fascination is there; it is strong; yet I think it is obvious. It grips one at the first. Of the many beautiful descriptions of it by gifted writers, it seems to me that the best are written after just a glimpse of it; a few days in a tent, a few nights under the stars. I do not think the fascination lasts.

It is not the heat, nor the glare, nor the sandstorms, nor even the solitude, that become oppressive after a time; it is the utter deadness and the howling of the wind.

Annie A. Quibell, *A Wayfarer in Egypt* (1925)

Denon speaks of the pleasurable sensations daily excited by the delicious temperature of *Cairo*, causing *Europeans* who arrive with the intention of spending a few months in the place, to remain during the rest of their lives, without ever persuading themselves to leave. Few persons, however, with whom we associated, were disposed to acquiesce in the opinion of this very amiable writer. Those who are desirous of uninterrupted repose, or who are able to endure the invariable dullness which prevails in every society to which strangers are admitted, may, perhaps, tolerate, without murmuring, a short residence in the midst of this dull and dirty city. The effect, whether it be of climate, or of education, or of government, is the same among all the settlers in Egypt, except the *Arabs*, namely, a disposition to exist without exertion of any kind; to pass whole days upon beds and cushions; smoking, and counting beads. This is what *Maillet* termed *Le vrai génie Egyptienne*; and that it may be acquired by residing among the native inhabitants of *Cairo*, is evident from the appearance exhibited by *Europeans* who have passed some years in the city.

E. D. Clarke, *Travels in Various Countries of Europe, Asia, and Africa* (1818)

THE REDISCOVERY OF EGYPT

Throughout the Middle Ages Egypt was dominated by the Turks. As a result it was largely inaccessible to the Christians of Western Europe, although educated men of the Renaissance period would have learned about Egypt through the writings of Plutarch, Strabo and Herodotus and the occasional traveller confirmed the existence of the great monuments. Christian missionaries were established in Cairo by the seventeenth century, but their interest lay more in the relics of the early Coptic Church than in the glories of pagan Egypt.

Jean de Thevenot, a French traveller who visited Egypt in 1652, recorded a description of the Great Pyramid and of a stone sarcophagus 'entirely covered in idols and hieroglyphs' which he discovered near Saqqara. But like most other travellers of the time he explored only the delta region and the environs of Cairo. It was left to another Frenchman, Benoit de Maillet, consul-general in Cairo in the reign of Louis XIV, to write a comprehensive description of Egypt giving pride of place to the ancient monuments. His memoirs, published in 1735, bore the title *Description of Egypt, containing many strange Observations on the ancient and modern Geography of this Country, on its ancient Monuments, its Morals, Customs, the Religion of its Inhabitants, on its Animals, Trees, Plants.* Obviously determined to leave nothing out, Maillet gave the West the first illustration of a pyramid. His cross-section of the Great Pyramid is taller than it should be, but otherwise reasonably accurate.

Maillet was also the first to loot the monuments for the benefit of European museums and was prevented from shipping Pompey's column in Alexandria home as a tribute to his king purely by practical concerns! Much of what he sent home to his patron, the Comte de Caylus, is now in the Bibliothèque Nationale in Paris.

But strangely, we owe the great rediscovery of Ancient Egypt to Napoleon. Although travel to Egypt increased throughout the eighteenth century, it is with the landing of Napoleon's army in 1798 that modern Egyptology can be said to have begun. One of the French party was Baron Dominique Vivant Denon, founder of what is now the Louvre. A protégé of the future Empress Josephine, he was included in the mission to Egypt through her influence, despite the fact that he was fifty years old and would have to endure the harsh living conditions of a military campaign. But Denon was a remarkable man. In the course of his career, he managed to survive the Revolution, despite his aristocratic birth; to remain in favour under Napoleon; and to continue his official duties and his writing under the restored King Louis XVIII. He outlived both emperor and king, dying in 1825 at the age of seventy-eight.

His reports led Napoleon to commission a group of scholars to compile a massive *Description of Egypt* (comprising nine volumes of text and eleven of illustrations). This work, based on Denon's writing and skilled draughtsman-like illustrations, was published between 1809 and 1822 and made Egypt madly fashionable among the French. It soon ran to forty editions and was translated into both English and German. In the meantime, Nelson's victory at the Battle of the Nile had opened the country up to British visitors. What followed was a period of huge advances in scholarly understanding of the Egyptian civilisation, frequently accompanied by shameless looting of its treasures.

The most significant piece of booty carried off by the Europeans was the Rosetta Stone. Until Napoleon's soldiers discovered this slab of basalt at Rosetta, near Alexandria, in

1799, Western scholars had been baffled by the Egyptian hieroglyphics, which bore no resemblance to any language with which they were familiar. The Rosetta Stone, however, was inscribed in three scripts: hieroglyphics; the everyday Egyptian script known as demotic; and Greek, which scholars could read quite easily. The inscription helpfully stated that all three scripts said the same thing – thanking Ptolemy V, king of Egypt around 200 BC, for his gifts to the temples – and, armed with this information, scholars could at last begin to make sense of the hieroglyphics.

The principal code-breaker was yet another Frenchman, Jean-François Champollion, who recognised that some of the symbols used were phonetic while others were pictorial. The inscription on the Rosetta Stone gave him enough information to translate many hitherto indecipherable texts. His letter to Monsieur Dacier, *Secrétaire perpetuel de l'Académie royale des Inscriptions et Belles-Lettres, relatives à l'alphabet des hiéroglyphiques phonétiques*, explaining his discovery, is perhaps the single most important contribution to modern Egyptology. It is ironic that the defeat of Napoleon enabled the British to lay claim to the Rosetta Stone, which has resided ever since in the British Museum in London.

Having done his ground-breaking work at home in France, Champollion journeyed to Egypt in 1828 and, in the company of the Italian explorer Ippolito Rosellini, spent the next two years there. They travelled as far south as Abu Simbel, studying both the architecture and the inscriptions of the ancient sites and Champollion was able to write to Dacier, with an understandable hint of self-congratulation, 'Now that I have followed the course of the Nile from its mouth to the Second Cataract, I am in a position to tell you that we need change nothing in our *Lettre relative à l'alphabet des hiéroglyphiques phonétiques*; our alphabet is correct: it applies equally well to the Egyptian monuments built during the time of the Romans and the Ptolemies and – what is of much greater interest – to the inscriptions in all the temples, palaces and tombs dating from the time of the pharaohs.'

Champollion was one of the first to be horrified at the looting of tombs and destruction of monuments, and to recommend that excavations be officially controlled. But for many decades to come, considerations of self-interest and profit prevailed over the demands of scholarship and heritage.

Looting of tombs was an ancient practice – there are records of trials dating back to 2000 BC – but it reached a peak in the early part of the nineteenth century under the viceroy Mohammed Ali. Determined to modernise the country of which he was, in effect, in complete control, Mohammed Ali recruited European 'technicians' to help him develop industry in Egypt. These 'technicians' – many of them happy to turn their hand to any activity that would make them money – also became the agents of foreign consuls-general interested in acquiring antiquities for museums or private collections at home. Over a period of forty years, they organised the removal of a vast number of ancient treasures.

Although this trade in antiquities greatly facilitated the work scholars in Europe and elsewhere, it could not be allowed to continue indefinitely – even the monumental sites of Egypt were not inexhaustible. The end of the piracy came in the mid-nineteenth century when another Frenchman, Auguste Mariette, under the auspices of the new viceroy, Said Pasha, founded the Egyptian Antiquities Service. Pillaging did not stop overnight – it was too lucrative a business for that to happen – but Mariette was eventually able to exercise some measure of control and ensure that, for the most part, only licensed archaeologists removed treasures from his adopted country's greatest resource.

In 1817 the Italian Giovanni Battista Belzoni discovered the entrance to the Pyramid of Khafre. The excitement among the team must have been incredible:

...the first block of granite was discovered on February 28; the following day, March 1, we uncovered three blocks of the same stone, one on either side and one above [the first], and all inclined toward the centre. My hopes and expectations were raised by this discovery which I felt foretold of immediate success. Indeed, the next day, March 2, at noon, we finally reached the real entrance of the pyramid.

I looked with care. I even searched, and I saw nothing but temples, but walls covered with obscure emblems, but hieroglyphics which attested the ascendancy of priests who still seem to domineer over the ruins, and whose empire still possesses my imagination.

Dominique Vivant Denon,
Travels in Upper and Lower Egypt (1803)

The painting on the fine plaster [inside the tombs at Giza] is often more beautiful than could be expected, and occasionally exhibits the freshness of yesterday in perfect preservation. The subjects on the walls are usually representations of scenes from the life of departed persons, and seem mostly to place their riches, cattle, fish, boats, hunts and servants, before the eyes of the observer. Through them we became acquainted with every particular of their private life.

Richard Lepsius, *Discoveries in Egypt* (1853)

THE ANCIENT KINGDOMS

There were three great periods of Egyptian civilisation, known respectively as the Old, Middle and New Kingdoms. Each began with a strong ruler who united the diverse regions under his control and initiated a period of peace and prosperity. Each ended when a weaker ruler allowed his kingdom to fall victim to civil war or to be overrun by foreign powers.

The Old Kingdom dates from about 2613 to about 2160 BC, although in fact Upper and Lower Egypt had been united under the pharaoh Narmer as early as 3100 BC. It was Narmer who first established a capital at Memphis, near modern Cairo, and whose strength paved the way for nearly a thousand years of tranquillity.

Four dynasties ruled Egypt in the course of the Old Kingdom. Most scholars recognise thirty Egyptian dynasties (usually identified with Roman numerals), from the time of the unification of the country until the death of the last native Egyptian pharaoh, Nectanebo II, in 343 BC. Others add two further dynasties, extending the chronology to the death of Cleopatra in 30 BC. The start of a new dynasty normally meant that there had been a break in the continuous male line. For example, Snefru, the first pharaoh of the IVth dynasty, had married the daughter of his predecessor, Huni, who had no surviving sons. We owe much of our knowledge of the pharaohs – including the divisions of the dynasties – to the writings of the historian Manetho, who lived during the reign of Ptolemy I (305–282 BC). No complete record of Manetho's works survives, but he was obviously highly thought of by a number of writers of the early Christian era, who quoted him extensively.

During the Old Kingdom there were great advances in learning and in the arts, and in building and technology: this is the age of the pyramid builders (see page 74). The most famous of these was Khufu, also known as by the Greek form of his name, Cheops, who reigned from 2589–2566 BC. Manetho gives a very disparaging report of his character, accusing him of having conceived 'a contempt for the gods', although intriguingly he is said to have repented of this and compiled 'the Sacred Books, which the Egyptians hold in high esteem'. Sadly, no trace of these Sacred Books remains.

It was during the Old Kingdom that the pharaohs attained godlike status. Horus, son of Osiris and Isis, had been closely associated with the early pharaohs, who believed they were the god's representative on earth. But Khufu's son Djedefre (2566–2558 BC) was the first to be given the title 'son of Ra'.

All the pyramids of this period are remarkable; that of Unas (2375–2345), last pharaoh of the Vth Dynasty, also contained a major contribution to Egyptology: the so-called 'Pyramid Texts'. These were columns of hieroglyphics inscribed on the walls of the tomb. Once deciphered, they were found to contain 228 spells to help the soul of the deceased as he journeyed to and entered the afterlife. Such inscriptions were frequently used during the VIth Dynasty, and although no complete set has been found, over four hundred spells have been identified. During the Middle Kingdom these spells were replaced by the 'Coffin Texts', which served a similar purpose and were themselves replaced during the New Kingdom by the spells which now form *The Book of the Dead* (see pages 7 and 116).

A kingdom the size of Egypt needed a complex administrative system. In due course, more and more power fell into the hands of local officials, leading to fragmentation and the eventual collapse of the Old Kingdom. The leader strong enough to reunite the country emerged in the person of Mentuhotep I, who became first pharaoh of the Middle

Kingdom in about 2040 BC. Under the Middle Kingdom the Egyptians became prosperous traders and successful military campaigners, conquering the kingdom of Nubia (which today straddles the border between southern Egypt and Sudan). Mining and quarrying for gold and building stone expanded, as great temples and obelisks were built from Thebes to Heliopolis. The invasion of a people called the Hyksos ('desert princes'), from the desert regions to the north and east, brought this period of harmony to an end in about 1750 BC.

The Hyksos had sacked Memphis, so the New Kingdom needed a new capital. The chosen city was Thebes, some 500 miles further up the Nile, where an Egyptian dynasty had continued to rule while the Hyksos controlled the north of the country. It became the capital of the reunited kingdom in about 1550 BC. This heralded a period of military conquest and architectural glory: the Valley of the Kings became the burial place of pharaohs and their fabulous wealth. Many of the most famous of the pharaohs – Akhenaten and his wife Nefertiti (see page 13), Hatshepsut, Tutankhamen (see page 102), Ramesses the Great (see page 10) – belong to this period. Their names have come down to us because, like the pyramid builders of the Old Kingdom, they built spectacular monuments to their own glory.

Queen Hatshepsut was the only female of the Egyptian dynasties to rule in her own right. In a political alliance, she had been married to her half-brother, Tuthmosis II (1518–1504 BC). Tuthmosis died while in his thirties, leaving a young son whose mother was a harem-girl. Hatshepsut, named as regent during her stepson's minority, simply usurped the young Tuthmosis' claim and ruled for twenty years after her husband's death. She took such titles as 'King of Upper and Lower Egypt' and 'She who embraces Amun, the foremost of women'. A detail from the obelisk in the Temple of Amun at

Opposite. A pharaoh and his queen make offerings to Hathor.

Karnak portrays her as a man, and she was depicted elsewhere with a false beard and all the regalia of kingship.

Despite this unpromising start to his reign, Tuthmosis III survived his stepmother by over thirty years and carved out his own place in history. One twentieth-century Egyptologist described him as 'the Napoleon of Egypt'. It was under Tuthmosis' brilliant and fearless generalship that the Egyptian army marched north as far as Syria and captured three important cities in the space of five months. Inscriptions at Karnak, written by the royal archivist Thanuny, suggest that Tuthmosis' army conquered a total of 350 cities in the next eighteen years.

In the course of the next century, especially under Amenhotep III (father of Amenhotep IV who became better known as Akhenaten), Egypt was at its wealthiest – and its most stable. The arts flourished. Sumptuous statues in alabaster and quartz, and five huge commemorative scarabs inscribed with events of the first ten years of the king's reign are among the treasures that have survived from this time.

In about 1086 BC the kingdom fell to the Persians, who were succeeded by the Greeks and then the Romans, who ruled Egypt until the arrival of Islam in the seventh century AD. These centuries saw Egypt becoming the centre of learning for the classical world: Alexander the Great founded Alexandria in the fourth century BC and its library (frequently damaged by fire and finally destroyed in the seventh century AD) was the finest of its time. But with the fall of the Egyptian pharaohs, the great period of its civilisation – which had extended over two thousand years – was over.

The English poet Percy Bysshe Shelley (1792–1822), in his famous poem *Ozymandias*, used the example of the Egyptian monuments – which would have been well known to his fashionable readers – to represent the transitory nature of human achievement:

I met a traveller from an antique land
Who said: 'Two vast and trunkless legs of stone
Stand in the desert... Near them, on the sand,
Half sunk, a shattered visage lies, whose frown,
And wrinkled lip, and sneer of cold command,
Tell that its sculptor well those passions read
Which yet survive, stamped on these lifeless things,
The hand that mocked them, and the heart that fed:
And on the pedestal these words appear:
"My name is Ozymandias, king of kings:
Look on my works, ye Mighty, and despair!"
Nothing beside remains. Round the decay
Of that colossal wreck, boundless and bare
The lone and level sands stretch far away.'

This country is a palimpsest, in which the Bible is written over Herodotus, and the Koran over that.

Lady Duff Gordon

The French novelist Pierre Loti (1850–1923) was a sailor in his youth and travelled widely throughout his life. He wrote lovingly of life in Egypt, being equally captivated by its ancient past and its contemporary Muslim society.

In the maze of narrow, winding streets, beneath the endless, overhanging balconies in finely carved wood lattice-work, we are forced to slow our pace as we join the tightly packed throng of people and animals... An occasional encounter with the more delightful face of the Orient as, above the tiny houses decorated with *mashrabiya* and arabesques, you catch a sudden glimpse of tall minarets soaring skyward in the dusk.

The English poet and traveller Wilfrid Scawen Blunt (1840–1922) described the capital of Egypt as follows:

...the immense city of Cairo, with its citadels and towers, and walls, and minarets stretching away for miles, the splendid ancient city, and beyond it, modern Cairo, with its turmoil of tramways, railroads, and other modernities.

The Egyptian novelist Naguib Mahfouz, born in 1911, received the Nobel Prize for his services to literature. These are his recollections of Alexandria:

...the morning dew, the down of white clouds, slanting rays of sunlight washed by the rain, the heart of memories steeped in honey and tears.

Opposite. A priest, recognisable by his panther-skin robe, performs the ceremony of the opening of the mouth for a pharaoh shown wearing a striped head cloth and an elaborate crown of ram's horns, feathers and gold cobras.

THE GODS

The Ancient Egyptians worshipped a vast and confusing pantheon of gods. As with the Greek deities, there are tales of brothers marrying sisters, and of fierce rivalry between gods. When the 'established' religion came into contact with localised beliefs, the local god often came to be identified with his equivalent in the dominant pantheon, which meant that a number of names might be used to represent the same deity.

The patriarch and matriarch of the Egyptian pantheon were Geb, god of the earth and of vegetation, and his sister and consort Nut, the creator goddess, believed to swallow the sky every evening and allow it to pass through her body by dawn. The best known of their children were Osiris, Isis and Seth.

Osiris had a number of functions, but his most important role was as god of the underworld. The pharaohs believed they 'became' Osiris after death and many funerary prayers and offerings are dedicated to him. He married his sister, Isis, the mother goddess, but was murdered by his jealous brother Seth. According to legend Isis spent years searching for her husband's body, which was still sealed into a coffin that had been encased in the trunk of a tree at Byblos in Lebanon. Breathing life back into the body, she impregnated herself with Osiris' semen and bore a son, Horus. In art, Horus is often depicted as a falcon, or in human form with a falcon's head.

Meanwhile, Seth had also found Osiris' body and hacked it into fourteen pieces, which he scattered along the Nile Valley. The faithful Isis found all the pieces except the penis, which Seth had thrown to a crocodile. The places where she buried the pieces have become sanctuaries to Osiris: one of these was Abydos, which became the centre of his cult. Osiris himself is said to have come back to life in order to teach Horus to take his place, and the early pharaohs believed they were the earthly incarnations of Horus. Isis was thus seen as guarding the rightful line of succession of the gods and their representatives on earth, the pharaohs.

Seth's role in the Egyptian pantheon is a strange one. Often seen as the incarnation of all evil, he also took part in the ceremony of 'Uniting the Two Lands', depicted in limestone reliefs recovered near Memphis and now in the Cairo Museum. In these reliefs falcon-headed Horus faces Seth, shown with the head of a dog, and both are tying the symbolic plants of Lower and Upper Egypt to a sign which denotes unity. Here, Seth clearly represents Upper Egypt. He has also been shown working in harmony with Horus at the anointing of a pharaoh, pouring water over the king's head in what is obviously a symbolic rite. It appears that after the conflict between Seth and Horus had been resolved, the victorious Horus was able to offer his uncle an important – if secondary – place in the pantheon.

During the reigns of the Ptolemies, Osiris came to be identified with Serapis, the bull god, who – under Greek and Roman influence – was also linked with Zeus, Jupiter, Pluto and even, because of his healing powers, with Aesculapius, the god of medicine. The cult of the bull god, Apis, was an ancient one, known in Memphis from prehistoric times. The bull was a sign of divine procreativity and sacred animals were worshipped as the living incarnation of the god. When one died it was given the name Oserapis (Osiris-Apis) and was mummified and buried amid great public lamentation. The

Overleaf. The sem priest, wearing a panther skin, carries out rituals behind a heap of offerings. The dead queen, wearing the cobra head-dress, sits on a throne. Her mummified form stands behind her.

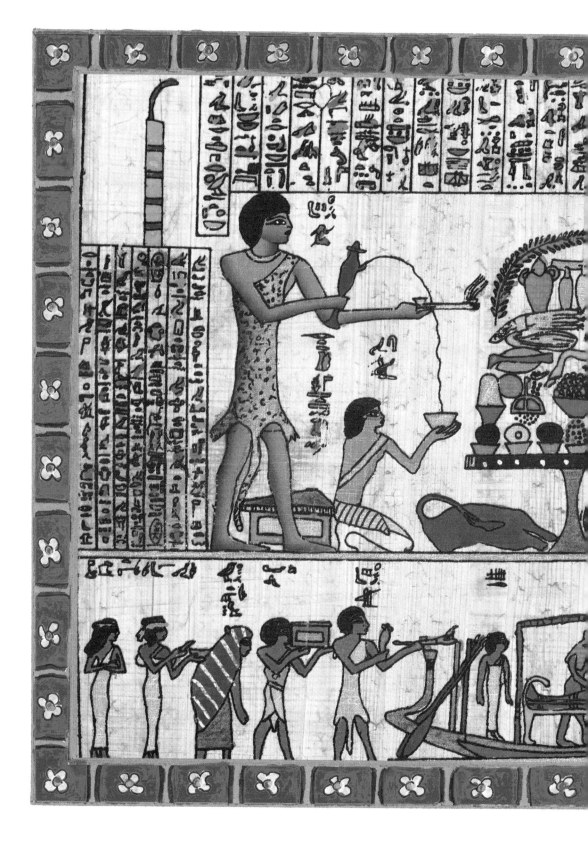

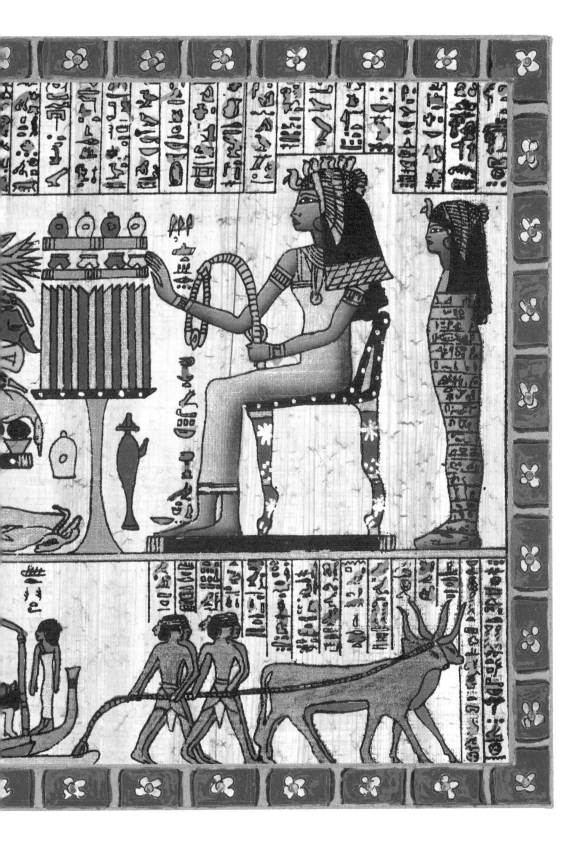

temple of Serapis, or Serapeum, at Memphis, was the great discovery of the founder of the Egyptian Antiquities Service, Auguste Mariette.

Osiris was also closely linked with Ra or Re, the creator and sun god, whose chariot rolled across the sky by day and disappeared into the underworld at night. Later pharaohs described themselves as 'sons of Ra'. In Thebes he was associated with a local god, Amun, to become known as Amun-Ra.

Perhaps because of his connection with the underworld, Ra was regarded with a considerable amount of fear. One of his symbols was a cobra, suggesting his ability to deliver instant retribution when necessary. On the other hand, his daughter Bastet, the protector of women and children, was seen as a benign goddess whose influence caused the corn to ripen. Often depicted in the form of a cat, she was the reason Egyptians considered that animal to be sacred.

A brief diversion in the worship of Ra occurred during the reign of Akhenaten (Amenhotep IV, 1350–1334 BC). He introduced a new monotheistic cult of the sun's disc, the Aten, in honour of whom he changed his own name. In a move that was at least partly political, he declared himself the only person who could communicate with the Aten, greatly offending the powerful existing priesthood. He also built a temple to Aten adjacent to the temple of Amun-Ra at Thebes, suppressing the cult of the latter. The worship of the Aten is one of the earliest examples of monotheism but did not long survive Akhenaten's death. Indeed, there was a violent backlash against the cult and Ra emerged once again as the focus of sun-worship.

Also connected with the afterlife were Anubis, the jackal-headed god of the dead who superintended the embalming of pharaohs and courtiers; and Thoth, the god of scribes and learning, depicted with the head of an ibis. He is said to have invented hieroglyphic writing, arithmetic and the calendar. A scrupulously fair god, he was responsible for recording the souls of the dead as they passed into the afterlife.

Egyptian funerary rites were complex, based on the belief that the spiritual and physical elements of the dead were reunited in the afterlife. This meant that the body itself had to be preserved. Embalming was the process which prevented corpses from decomposing. Internal organs were removed and preserved in what were known as Canopic jars, identified by having a representation of the head of the deceased as a lid. Aromatic drugs helped delay the process of decay, as did wrapping the body tightly in bandages. Embalming was a ritual as well as a skill, with the embalmers reciting prescribed prayers at each stage of the procedure.

The resulting 'mummy' – the bandaged figure – was placed inside a casket with a door painted on the outside to enable the dead to observe the world of the living. Funeral processions escorted the dead to their tomb, where they were buried accompanied by objects which would facilitate their journey to the next world and make them comfortable in the afterlife. Excavations of pyramids and other tombs have found signs of food and clothing as well as furniture, household utensils, ornaments and even, in the case of the pharaohs, lavishly decorated gold thrones. Inscriptions on tombs depicted events from the life of the deceased and contained prayers and spells for his safe passage into the next world.

The other major preoccupation of the Ancient Egyptians was growing sufficient food to feed themselves, which depended on the annual flooding of the Nile. A number of their deities were therefore concerned with grain, the harvest and the river itself. Osiris was sometimes worshipped as a grain god: in that case he was depicted as or with a sack from which emerged sprouting seed. Paintings of Osiris often show him with green skin, presumably because of his connection with fertility.

The god of the Nile was Hapy, whose arrival, in the form of the annual flood, heralded the start of a period of plenty. His retinue included crocodile gods and frog goddesses. Sobek, the crocodile god, controlled the water and marshes of the Nile and represented the might of the pharaohs. A sanctuary near Aswan shows him as the consort of Hathor, the goddess of love, dancing and music, sometimes depicted with a cow's head, as a symbol of motherly love, but also depicted as a beautiful woman.

The Egyptian habit of identifying animals with deities intrigued writers from other cultures. Herodotus writing in the fifth century BC, recorded the varying attitudes to crocodiles:

Some of the Egyptians hold crocodiles sacred; others do not do so, but treat them as enemies. The dwellers about Thebes and the lake Moeris deem them to be very sacred. There, in every place one crocodile is kept, trained to be tame; they put ornaments of glass and gold on its ears and bracelets on its forefeet, provide for it special food and offerings, and give the creatures the best of treatment while they live; after death the crocodiles are embalmed and buried in sacred coffins. But about Elephantine they are not held sacred, and are even eaten.

Memphis ... contains temples, one of which is that of Apis, who is the same as Osiris; it is here that the bull Apis is kept in a kind of sanctuary, being regarded, as I have said, as god; his forehead and certain other small parts of his body are marked with white, but the other parts are black; and it is by these marks that they always choose the bull suitable for the succession, when the one that holds the honour has died. In front of the sanctuary is situated a court, in which there is another sanctuary belonging to the bull's mother. Into this court they set Apis loose at a certain hour, particularly that he may be shown to foreigners; for although people can see him through the window in the sanctuary, they wish to see him outside also; but when he has finished a short bout of skipping in the court they take him back again to his familiar stall.

Strabo, *Geography* (1st century BC)

The greatest festival was that of Osiris. The priests covered a golden ox with a fine coat of black linen, and exhibited it from the 17th to 20th Athyr (14th-17th Nov.), mourning for the fall of the Nile, the end of the north winds, the shortened day, and the leafless trees, but planting in hope of new growth. Six months later...they go to the seaside with a shrine in which is a small vessel of gold; in this they pour some fresh water and then cry aloud 'Osiris is found.' They then mix some soil with spices and incense, and work it up into the form of a crescent, which they afterwards dress and adorn.

Sir William Flinders Petrie, *Religious Life in Ancient Egypt* (1924)

The triumph of priesthood at Heliopolis, founding the Vth dynasty, is marked by long lists of lands given by each king to the temple. In the VIth dynasty, the priesthood were gaining exemption from taxation in kind and in labour, and publishing their immunities by s etting up their title deeds at the entrances to the temples. In the Old Kingdom, the principal temple building was f or worship of the king; the temples of deities – even at Abydos – were small brick structures, the gateways, only, being built of stone.

Sir William Flinders Petrie, *Religious Life in Ancient Egypt* (1924)

Abydos was the holiest place in Egypt, sanctified by the graves of the ancient kings that lie out on the desert, near the gorge where their father Ra sinks to rest in the western mountains, sanctified even more by the legend that there the god Osiris, who died and rose again, lay buried after his brother slew him. It is hardly possible to disentangle the primitive part of this tale from those of later mythology that gathered round it, but there is little doubt that all the higher side of Egyptian religion was bound up with the Abydos worship and that the mysteries celebrated there did set forth the resurrection from the dead and the judgments in the world to come.

Annie A. Quibell, *A Wayfarer in Egypt* (1925)

Opposite. A queen pays homage to Hathor.

The transit of the soul to the blessed west of Osiris began at Abydos, up the long valley which leads to the Oasis road. The soul is represented setting out sturdily, staff in hand, to begin its long march. The Oasis was the frontier of the unknown. Beyond that lay the end of the world, at the mountains where the sun left the visible world to enter the underworld of stars... There the fertile isles would be reached, where the corn grew higher than any on earth and uninterrupted blessings awaited the soul.

Sir William Flinders Petrie, *Religious Life in Ancient Egypt* (1924)

The Apis Bull is the calf of a cow which is never able after to have another. The Egyptians believe that a flash of lightning strikes the cow from heaven, and thus causes her to conceive the Apis. It has distinctive marks. It is black, with a white diamond on its forehead, the image of an eagle on its back, two white hairs on its tail and a scarab-beetle mark under its tongue.

Herodotus, *History* (5th century BC)

Three thousand years had had no effect upon [the Serapeum, burial place of the Apis bulls]. The fingermarks of the last Egyptian who put the last stone in place, were still visible in the mud plaster. In a corner, bare feet had left their mark in soft mud. Nothing had been disturbed.

Auguste Mariette (1851)

In a word, to form a true idea of so much magnificence, [the reader] ought to believe himself dreaming while he reads, for that the traveller believes himself dreaming while he sees [the Temple of Karnak].

Dominique Vivant Denon,
Travels in Upper and Lower Egypt (1803)

How beautiful, how grand the approach to Luxor must have been, when these Obelisks stood before the colossal statues of Remeses II, one on either side of the approach to the stupendous pylons, enriched with sculpture and painting, by which the Temple was entered!

William Brockendon, note to David Roberts'
Egypt and Nubia (1855-6)

The Serapeum excavation had aroused all my dormant fighting instincts. Back in France, I tried to battle with some text or other, to convince myself that this was what science was all about; but I could not...
I began thinking about a new project at Thebes and in the necropolis at Abydos, or drafting a dissertation on the scientific value of setting up a protection service for ancient monuments (one which I would, of course, direct). I would have died or gone mad if there had not been an opportunity for me to return to Egypt more or less immediately.

Auguste Mariette, *Letter* (1850s)

It is impossible to imagine the impression created by this vast underground passageway, whose lighting, so arranged, has a strange, dreamlike quality...Leading off the gallery are lateral chambers housing the immense sarcophagi of the Apis Bulls. Each of these was lit up too...whichever way you turn, the effect is truly magical.

A visitor to the Serapeum (1850s)

Giovanni Battista Belzoni left us this impression of Abu Simbel:

In front of the small temple are six colossi which are more impressive from a distance than close to. They are about thirty feet high and carved out of the rock like the great temple, which is decorated with a huge statue whose head and shoulders alone are visible above the sand. I could see even from a long way off that it was superbly carved. A row of hieroglyph runs along the frieze.

On the morning of the third day Abu Simbel came in sight. In the farthest mountain in the group there was a piece cut out; and then two such places appeared, the larger being the entrance to the King's Temple, the other the entrance to the Queen's. We landed at a difficult spot where you have to climb the escarpment on all fours; and then you stand before the four giants and feel for the first moment oppressed by the strangeness of your company. Including their crowns they must be a good twenty metres high, and as their feet stand on bases you can hardly reach their toes. They sit quietly there, two and two, on either side of the

entrances which begin below their knees, and are all carved
– lock, stock, and barrel – out of the grey stone of the
mountain. The facade is otherwise confined to the flat
rectangular piece before which the colossi sit, and to a bit
of ornament at the upper edge. The upper part of one
giant's body has been knocked away, and the others are
shamefully pitted; you can still imagine, however, what they
once looked like, and the damage has not impaired their
grandeur. They are very large, twelve times lifesize; and you
can work out where the heads would reach to if it occurred
to them to stand up. In the photograph, however, which we
were once shown in the institute at Cairo, they were quite
disproportionately bigger. Let me warn you for the ten-
thousandth time to beware of photographs.

Julius Meier-Graefe, *Pyramid and Temple* (1934)

Surrounded by bodies, by heaps of mummies in all directions,
which, previous to my being accustomed to the sight,
impressed me with horror. The blackness of the wall, the
faint light given by the candles and torches for want of air,
the different objects that surrounded me, seeming to converse
with each other, and the Arabs with the candles or torches in
their hands, naked and covered with dust, themselves
resembling living mummies absolutely formed a scene that
cannot be described.

Giovanni Belzoni, c. 1817, quoted in M. W. Disher,
Pharaoh's Fool (1957)

*Opposite. A queen offering incense to the gods. She wears
the royal vulture head-dress, topped by plumes and a
solar disc.*

I suppose the common houses of the ancients, in these warm countries, were constructed of very slight materials, after they left their caves in the mountains. There was indeed no need for any other. Not knowing the regularity of the Nile's inundation, they never could be perfectly secure in their own minds against the deluge, and this slight structure of private buildings seems to be the reason so few of these ruins are found in the many cities once built in Egypt. If there ever were any other buildings, they must now be covered with the white sand from the mountains; for the whole plain to the foot of these is overflowed, and in cultivation.

James Bruce, *Travels to Discover the Source of the Nile* (1804)

Midday, in unexpected heat, at the temple of Es Sebua. An avenue of Rameses statues and sphinxes... On one of the reliefs the colour is partly preserved: brick-red and lemon-yellow – Van Gogh's palette. It is odd what a touch of colour suggests! The Copts have made a church out of the temple; or tried to make one, with a dour protestant entrance, and have painted over the old reliefs with Christian saints who haven't lasted. Egypt is always breaking through.

Julius Meier-Graefe, *Pyramid and Temple* (1934)

The moon shines like the midnight sun; a scorpion or a snake making its way across the sand would be as

clearly visible now as if bathed in the fierce rays of Ra himself. It's an unearthly light, soft silver with sepia shadows. I can distinguish pebbles over which my camel plods, his soft pads enveloping them like dough. He makes a shuffling noise like the buffing of old leather. The silence is intense... Circling the Great Pyramid we wind our way over Memphis' ruined necropolis.
A slight breeze has risen, driving in off the Nile it cools the air, but the great tumbled boulders of temples and tombs are still hot from the sun, we can feel the heat radiating from them as we ride by.

Roderick Cameron, *My Travel's History* (1950)

27 March 1850. Abu Simbel. The colossi. Effect of the sun seen through the door of the large temple half blocked by sand: as though through an air-hole.
At the far end, three colossi half visible in the shadow. Lying on the ground and blinking. I had the impression that the first colossus on the right was moving its eyelids. Handsome heads, ugly feet.
The bats utter their sharp little cry. For a moment some other animal made a regular sound: it was like a country clock striking in the distance. I thought of Norman farms in summer, when everyone is in the fields, towards three in the afternoon...and of King Mykerinos riding in his chariot one evening around Lake Moeris with a priest beside him; he tells him of his love for his daughter. This is a harvest evening...the buffalo are coming home.

Gustave Flaubert, *Travel Notes*

THE PYRAMIDS

The pyramids were funeral monuments to the pharaohs of the Old Kingdom. In them were buried not only the dead king, but members of his family and court and all the money, household goods and servants he would need to take with him on his journey into the afterlife. The oldest surviving pyramid is also the oldest surviving building in the world made entirely of stone. This is the step pyramid at Saqqara, tomb of Djoser, the second pharaoh of the Old Kingdom, who died in 2649 BC. Like other pyramids, its interior is a maze of tunnels and chambers, including several burial chambers and surrounded by a mortuary complex which included a life-size limestone statue of Djoser.

Earlier tombs had been flat benchlike structures called *mastabas*. The step pyramid emerged as a result of piling six *mastabas*, each smaller than the last, on top of each other, to give the spirit of the dead a larger area in which to roam. The decoration of the mortuary complex shows Djoser performing rituals which demonstrate his fitness to rule; it has been suggested that his entrails were buried in the separate South Tomb, symbolising the fact that Djoser was king of both Lower and Upper Egypt.

The most famous of all the pyramids is the Great Pyramid at Giza. The burial place of Khufu or Cheops, who died in 2566 BC, it is the only survivor of the Seven Wonders of the Ancient World. Until the nineteenth century AD it was the tallest manmade structure in the world, originally 481 feet high, although it has now lost the top 30 feet. It is estimated that it took 100,000 men more than 20 years to build. Much of the

Opposite. A lady gathering fruit in an orchard.

stone is local limestone, but the chambers are lined with red granite, which must have been brought down the river from Aswan, some 500 miles away. It used 2.3 million blocks with an average weight of 2.5 tons, and covers an area of over 13 acres. The outer casing was Tura limestone, laid over the structure from the top down and almost entirely stripped during the Middle Ages to build the city of Cairo. Herodotus claimed that the building of the pyramid cost about 1600 silver talents – about £5 million.

Among the most fascinating items discovered in the Great Pyramid were the remains of a magnificent ship made of cedarwood. This elegant craft would have been intended to convey Khufu to the afterlife. It was 141 feet long – too long for the pit dug to hold it – so it had been painstakingly taken apart into over a thousand pieces.

Khufu's mother Hetep-heres was among the other royals buried in his pyramid, and her burial chamber revealed more evidence of the Egyptian concern to provide the dead with practical necessities for the afterlife. Hetep-heres' sarcophagus was accompanied by armchairs and a bed, vases, jewellery and even a gold manicure set.

No one really understands how the Great Pyramid was built, nor why Khufu chose this site, rather than Saqqara or his father's burial place at Dahshur. Nor do we know why, having chosen the site, he did not build on the highest point – he left that privilege to one of his sons, with the result that the nearby Pyramid of Khafre looks, by virtue of its location, to be the taller of the two. But these unanswered questions merely add to the mystique of the pyramids.

Khafre's pyramid, known as the Second Pyramid at Giza, also contains vast slabs of Aswan granite and, unlike its more famous neighbour, retains some of the limestone casing. A vast polished statue of Khafre himself, remarkably well preserved, with the back of his headdress protected by the falcon-god Horus, is one of the finest survivors of the ancient world.

The world-famous Sphinx forms part of the Khafre pyramid complex; its face is believed to be that of Khafre. Some 66 feet high and 240 feet long, it was carved out of local limestone. According to Greek legend the Sphinx was a lion-like creature with a human head which killed anyone who could not answer its riddle. At Giza the statue is said to represent Ra, the sun god, at the time of his rising in the east at dawn.

Around AD 672, the Irish monk Fidelis visited the Pyramids while on his way to the Holy Land with a group of fellow monks. This journey was related by Dicuil, another Irish monk, author of *Mensura Terrae*:

...After a long voyage on the Nile, they saw in the distance the Granaries made by Saint Joseph. There were seven of them to match the number of years of plenty: they looked like mountains, four in one place and three in another... [They] had a careful look at the three granaries, and were once more amazed that from their foundation right up to their topmost point they were made entirely of stone. The lower part of them was rectangular, but the upper part was round, and the very top was as sharp as a needle. This brother [Fidelis] measured one side of these granaries, and it was four hundred paces from corner to corner.

The pyramids gave me an overwhelming sense of vastness as an abstract quality, quite divorced from their physical existence, and this I think is the cause of their ability to inspire strange and nameless fears.

Richard Carrington, *The Tears of Isis* (1959)

I do not believe that the Egyptians came into being at the same period as the Delta; on the contrary, they have existed ever since Mankind appeared on earth, and as the Delta increased with the passage of time, many of them moved into the new territory and many remained where they originally were.

Herodotus, *History* (5th century BC)

Think of it, soldiers; from the summit of these pyramids, forty centuries look down upon you.

Napoleon Bonaparte to his Army of Egypt, 1798

Time fears the pyramids. After consideration of these pyramids, one is forced to comprehend the combined efforts of the most intelligent men...that the most learned axioms of geometry were called upon to show in these wonders the vast extent of human ability.

Abdul Latif, 12th century

A laborious walk in the flaming sun brought us to the foot of the Great Pyramid of Cheops. It was a fairy vision no longer. It was a corrugated, unsightly mountain of stone. Each of its monstrous steps was a wide stairway which rose upward, step above step, narrowing as it went, till it tapered to a point far aloft in the air. Insect men and women … were creeping about its dizzy perches, and one little black swarm were waving postage stamps from the airy summit – handkerchiefs will be understood.

Mark Twain, *The Innocents Abroad* (1875)

It is impossible to convey to anyone who has not seen the Great Pyramid either a proper conception of its size, or of the emotions experienced as one stands at its foot.

Richard Carrington, *The Tears of Isis* (1959)

Inside the Great Pyramid. Suddenly, the corridor rose steeply, The torch illuminated an imposing gallery, about 26 feet high with corbeled upper courses. Breathing became easier and we might have been at the entrance to a magnificent temple were it not for the steps carved in this slippery slope. But they were only shallow notches about three feet apart and we advanced with great difficulty, often falling, unless supported by the Beduins who climbed like cats along this eerie corridor.

Opposite. A recumbent Anubis, the god of the dead who watched over the embalming process. Large effigies of this type guarded the open doorway from the burial chamber into the Treasury in Tutankhamun's tomb.

The dry stone blocks are so marvellously positioned that you would not get a pin between them.

Edouard Schuré

With respect to the interior of the pyramid, it is so dim, and the walls are so blackened by the smoke from candles burnt there by visitors over the centuries, that it is difficult to judge the quality of the stones ... What one does notice is that they are highly polished, extraordinarily hard and so perfectly joined that it would be impossible to slide a knife point in the space that lies between them.

Benoit de Maillet, *Description of Egypt* (1735)

I know that philosophers may groan or smile at the thought that the greatest monument ever created by mankind is a tomb; but why see the Pyramid of Cheops merely as a pile of stones and a skeleton?

François René de Chateaubriand (1768–1848)

View of the Sphinx... The gray of the sand, the Pyramids and the sphinx are steeped in a rosy hue; in the intensely blue sky eagles glide and circle slowly round the summits.

Gustave Flaubert, *Travel Notes* (1850)

The well-known triangular forms look small and shadowy, and are too familiar to be in any way startling ... It is only in approaching them, and observing how they grow with every foot of the road, that one begins to feel they are not so familiar after all ... one discovers that it was with the forms of the Pyramids, and only their forms, that one had been acquainted all these years past ... Standing there close against the base of it; touching it; measuring her own height against one of its lowest blocks; looking up all the stages of that vast, receding, rugged wall, which leads upward like an Alpine buttress and seems almost to touch the sky, the Writer suddenly became aware ... Now, for the first time, they resolved themselves into something concrete, definite, real.

Amelia Edwards, *A Thousand Miles Up the Nile* (1877)

The French painter and author Eugène Fromentin (1820–76) provides us with this 'view from the deck':

As the Nile widens out once again and flows between the slopes of Jebel Mogattam and a curtain of date palms, all the pyramids are visible. The Pyramid of Giza is almost out of sight, the old Pyramid of Saqqara is level with the boat and the Pyramids of Dashur are drawing closer. Cairo has completely disappeared.

As every thing that is regular is small or great only by comparison ... the spectator is astonished to feel within himself an abatement of that impression which [the Pyramids] had produced while at a distance; but as soon as he begins to measure by a known scale these gigantic productions of art, they recover all their immensity ... We have an example of comparison in Europe, in the church of St Peter at Rome, of which the harmony of the proportions, or rather the graduation of the lines, conceals the height, the idea of which is not restored till, lowering the eyes on some priests going to say mass ... we imagine that we see a group of puppets.

Dominique Vivant Denon,
Travels in Upper and Lower Egypt (1803)

The beauty of the land and the legacy of its history seem insignificant when compared with the magnificence of the evening sky which I awaited as if it were the sole event of the day.

Edouard Schuré

The wickedness of Cheops reached to such a pitch that, when he had spent all his treasures and wanted more, he sent his daughter to the stews, with orders to procure him a certain sum – how much I cannot say, for I was not told; she procured it, however, and at the same time, bent on leaving a

Opposite. A queen making an offering to Osiris with Isis and Nephtus behind him. Isis was the sister as well as the wife of Osiris, and the mother of Horus, who is usually represented as a falcon. She symbolised the perfect mother. Nephtus was the sister of Isis and Osiris, the mother of Anubis, who is often shown as a jackal.

monument which should perpetuate her own memory, she required each man to make her a present of a stone towards the works which she contemplated. With these stones she built the pyramid which stands mid-most of the three that are in front of the Great Pyramid, measuring along each side a hundred and fifty feet.

Herodotus, *History* (5th century BC)

The whole ground was thick with...pottery, and it seemed almost a sacrilege to walk over the heaps with the fine lustrous black ware crunching beneath one's boots... It seemed as if I were wandering in the smashings of the Museum vase-rooms... Very precious was this rubbish to me, layer under layer of broken vases, from the innumerable small bowls to the great craters of noble size and design; and most precious of all were the hundreds of dedications inscribed on the pottery...altogether far outnumbering all our past material for the archaic alphabets.

William Flinders Petrie, *Ten Years' Digging in Egypt* (1881–91)

'Les Pyramides? Ça, c'est au bout du tramway,' said a French lady to a friend of mine, unconsciously voicing the point of view of a great many Cairene residents, who look upon the Pyramid plateau as a good place for an excursion, perfectly oblivious of the fact that there may be something to be looked for there of a different order of interest.

I suppose it must have been much more impressive to see the Pyramids thirty or forty years ago, when there was no tram and one went by carriage from Cairo, or better still, when there was no road and no Nile bridge, and one crossed in a ferry boat to Giza and rode out the six miles from there on donkeys or camels. But it is a standing marvel to me how little all the changes have been able to vulgarize the place. The electric tramway stops beside the big hotel at the foot of the slope, motors hoot up it and deposit their burdens at the very base of the Great Pyramid; a regular Bank-holiday crowd of Levantines pours out from Cairo every Sunday, and yet, hardly do we pass round the corner of the pyramid than the silence of the desert gets hold of us. It is very good to get away from the guides and the dragomans and think about it quietly. Perhaps the best thing of all is to stay out at Mena House or to camp near by and so be able to go about and see the morning lights, the sunset and the moon, and grow familiar with the mighty cemetery in all its aspects, but one can make excellent expeditions from Cairo by taxi or tram, and there is nothing more rewarding.

Annie A. Quibell, *A Wayfarer in Egypt* (1925)

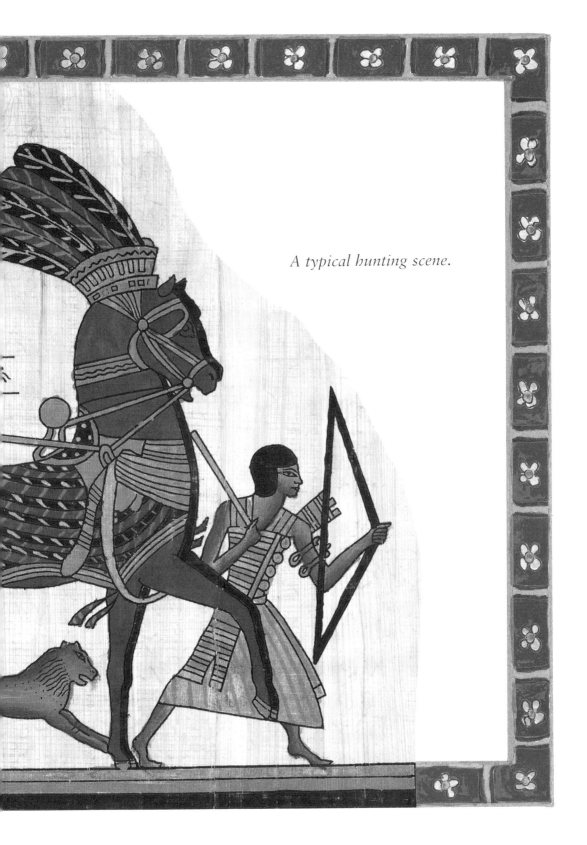

A typical hunting scene.

ARTS & SCIENCE

Every one of the surviving monuments of Ancient Egypt bears witness to the Egyptians' extraordinary knowledge of science and the decorative arts. The Pyramids could not possibly have been built without architects well versed in physics and mathematics; while the adornment of temples and the artefacts found in tombs are irrefutable evidence of the taste of those who commissioned them and the skill of the craftsmen who executed them. Talented painters, sculptors, carpenters and goldsmiths abounded, and most of them were employed in large workshops controlled by the pharaoh, the government or a temple, to carry out huge projects for the greater glory of the individual, the state or the gods.

One of the greatest of Egyptian architects attained the status of a god himself. Imhotep, chief vizier to the Pharaoh Djoser (2668–2649 BC), was responsible for the design of the step pyramid at Saqqara. He seems to have been much respected during his lifetime: an inscription at the base of a statue of Djoser describes him as 'The Treasurer of the King of Lower Egypt, the First after the King of Lower Egypt, Administrator of the Great Palace, Hereditary Lord, the High Priest of Heliopolis, Imhotep the builder, the sculptor, the maker of

Opposite. The hawk-headed god Ra, the sun god, appears on the right. The Ancient Egyptians were fascinated by the scarab – a dung beetle – which had the ability to move balls of dung much larger than its body, by rolling them along. They believed that Ra rolled the sun across the sky each day in a similar fashion. Ra came to be identified with Amun, a popular deity of Thebes, and the resulting new god was worshipped as Amun-Ra.

stone vases...' It is little wonder that he should later have been deified as a god of wisdom.

Egyptian painting was largely religious or commemorative in nature, perhaps because the Egyptians endowed their art with a certain magical power: a statue of a deity, person or animal, with suitable inscription, could provide a home for the spirit of the depicted being. A tomb painting portraying the deceased enjoying the pleasures of this world ensured that the pleasures remained available in the afterlife. Animals were frequently included in paintings, usually because they were identified with one of the many deities – the jackal with Anubis, the ibis with Thoth and the goose with Hapy, for example.

The depiction of people followed strict stylistic conventions. The central figure of a painting – the god or monarch – is shown with all essential features visible. Thus the head is in profile, although the eye almost faces the onlooker; the shoulders are front on and the upper part of the torso in profile. The main figures are usually seated, static and calm, while their servants are seen to bustle about around them.

Gold and semi-precious stones were plentiful in Egypt; jewellers, goldsmiths and ornament makers of every kind flourished throughout the pharaonic period. Beads, amulets, decorated bowls and vases, intricate inlay work and marquetry in gold, bronze, alabaster, porcelain, quartzite, ivory, cornelian and decorative glass have all survived. Even weapons were adorned with tales of prowess: a bronze inlaid axe-head from the time of the XVIIIth dynasty shows the pharaoh Ahmose (1570–1546 BC) executing a rebel, presumably to incite its owner to similar acts of bravery. Copper was used for tools and jewellery from the earliest times, though silver did not occur naturally in Egypt: it must have been imported, perhaps from Syria, for a wall painting at Thebes dating from the fifteenth century BC depicts Syrian chiefs offering vases of gold and silver to the pharaoh Sobekhotep; and the Roman historian Tacitus quotes a priest who visited Egypt in 19 BC and referred to the tributes the subject people paid to Rome: 'the weight of gold and silver, the numbers of weapons and horses, the temple-offerings of ivory and spices, the quantities of corn and other materials contributed by every country'.

Music and dance were an essential accompaniment to the sumptuous banquets held by the wealthy, and to the worship of the gods. String and wind instruments resembling the modern harp and flute were known, as was a form of drum made from skin or parchment drawn tight over a pottery frame. Dancers might enhance their performance by wearing or carrying bells, rattles or cymbals.

Much of what we know of Egyptian culture has come down to us in the form of hieroglyphics, the pictorial writing with which the Egyptians embellished their monuments. Hieroglyphics usually represented people, animals or events, which sometimes told a story and sometimes – as with the letters of our own alphabet – indicated a sound. The pictures were carefully executed by skilled craftsmen. In addition to this rather complicated way of conveying a message, the Egyptians had a more cursive script, better suited to brush and ink writing on papyrus, which they used for documents and lesser inscriptions.

In the course of her journey through Egypt in 1848, the English writer Harriet Martineau (1802–76) gave us this description of the Ramesseum, the monumental complex built by Ramesses II in his capital of Thebes, on the West Bank of the Nile:

It is melancholy to sit on the piled stones amidst the wreck of this wonderful edifice, where violence inconceivable to us has been used to destroy what art inconceivable to us had erected.

The traveller is ill equipped who goes through Egypt without something more than a mere guide-book knowledge. In the desolation of Memphis, in the shattered splendour of Thebes, he sees only the ordinary pathos of ordinary ruins. As for Abou Simbel, the most stupendous historical record ever transmitted from the past to the present, it tells him but a half-intelligible story. Holding to the merest thread of explanation, he wanders from hall to hall, lacking altogether the potent charm of foregone association which no Murray can furnish.

Amelia Edwards, *A Thousand Miles Up the Nile* (1877)

Opposite. The eighteenth-dynasty king Akhenaten (1350–1334 BC) and his queen, Nefertiti, with three of their six daughters. Akhenaten introduced the mono-theistic cult of Aten, the sun disc.

The greatest loss in the break-up of the Egyptian civilisation was that of the literature. We have only recovered a minute part of the whole private literature, in tales, letters, and accounts. Of the official records and laws there are but a few temple inscriptions, and a very scanty outline to show what is gone. Clemens states that there were forty-two rolls of Thoth [the god of learning], 'treated by the Egyptians with the most profound respect, and carried in their religious processions. First came the singer, holding two in his hands, one containing hymns in honour of the gods, the other, rules for the conduct of the monarch. Next to him, the horoscopist, whose duty it was to recite the four books of astrology, one of which treated of the fixed stars, another of solar and lunar eclipses, and the remaining two of the rising of the sun and moon. Ten books containing those things which related to the gods and the religion of Egypt, as sacrifices, first-fruits, hymns, prayers, processions, holy days, and the like. Last of all came the prophet, with ten other books, called sacerdotal, relating to the laws, the gods, and rules of the priesthood. Thus, then, of the forty-two most useful books of Thoth, thirty-six contained all the philosophy of Egypt, and the last six treated of medicine, anatomy, and the cure of diseases.'

Sir William Flinders Petrie,
Religious Life in Ancient Egypt (1924)

Opposite. Queen Nefertiti. This picture is based on the famous bust found at Amarna in 1913 and now in the Berlin Museum. It captures her delicate beauty and typifies the new, more realistic style introduced by the sculptor Thutmose and other artists who worked for Akhenaten's court.

The writer Andrée Chedid, in her book *Nefertiti and Akhenaten's Dream*, tells of the Pharaoh Akhenaten's doomed capital of El Amarna:

Each of these streets...was conceived, traced by Akhenaten. We watched, together, as each of the buildings was constructed. Now, all I have to do is close my eyes and I see its towering temples and houses, its living gardens and its network of streets.

Their gold covering and their polished surfaces reflected on my own excited face so that it seemed as though I was looking into the faces of my own ancestors. One of them, that of a queen, smiled on me like an old friend.

Emile Brugsch in the Valley of the Kings (1881)

A few very beautiful pieces of sculpture have been found here [at El Amarna], others may yet be found, but never many. Such pieces are rare at any time, and for the short bloom of Tell el Amarna the quantity of work on the tombs must have occupied the artists completely. The tombs are in the cliffs, about three miles across the low desert. They were full of lovely scenes, but have suffered frightful damage...
From these tombs have come one or two versions of the Hymn to the Aten, a splendid religious poem, which in itself suffices to shed a glory over Akhenaten and his city.

Opposite. Akhenaten offering to Aten, whose beneficient sun rays extend their blessing hands over him and his family.

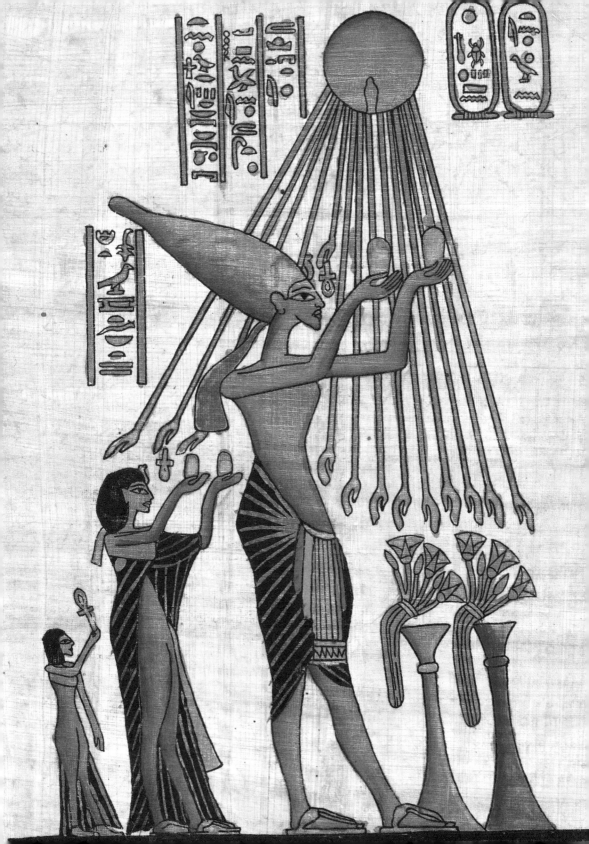

The grave of Akhenaten lies far up a lonely wady, so remote, one would think, that it would have been safe from wilful damage. But even here the sculptures have suffered terribly, probably from reprisals by the Amen priesthood after the return to the old worship. Akhenaten's body was not allowed to rest there. It was found about twenty years ago, in a tomb in the Valley of the Tombs of the Kings at Thebes, enclosed in a magnificent coffin, but with no funerary equipment, except four alabaster Canopic jars, each with his portrait on the lid. These are exquisite things; among the few great gems that have come down to us.

Annie A. Quibell, *A Wayfarer in Egypt* (1925)

The distinguished traveller James Bruce was struck by the evidence of Egyptian culture he found in a tomb in Thebes. In his *Travels to Discover the Source of the Nile* (1804), he wrote:

In one pannel were several musical instruments strowed upon the ground, chiefly of the hautboy kind, with a mouth-piece of reed. There were also some simple pipes, or flutes. With them were several jars apparently of potter's-ware, which, having their mouths covered with parchment, or skin, and being braced on their sides like a drum, were probably the instrument called the *tabor*, or *tabret*, beat upon by the hands, coupled in the earliest ages with the harp, and preserved still in Abyssinia, though its companion, the last mentioned instrument, is no longer known there.

In three following pannels were painted, in fresco, three harps, which merited the utmost attention, whether we consider the elegance of these instruments in their form, and the detail of their parts, as they are here clearly expressed, or confine ourselves to the reflection that necessarily follows, to how great perfection music must have arrived, before an artist could have produced so complete an instrument as either of these.

Early, however, as the papyrus was known, it does not appear to me ever to have been a plant that could have existed in the Nile, or, as authors have said, been proper to it. Its head is too heavy, and, in a plain country, the wind must have had too violent a hold of it. The stalk is small and feeble, and likewise too tall, the root too short and slender to stay it against the violent pressure of the wind and current, therefore I believe it never could be a plant growing in the Nile itself, or in any very deep or rapid river.

Pliny, who seems to have considered and known it perfectly in all its parts, does not pretend that it ever grew in the body of the Nile, but in the calishes or places where the Nile overflowed and was stagnant, and where the water was not above two cubits high.

James Bruce, *Travels to Discover the Source of the Nile* (1804)

THE VALLEY OF
THE KINGS

The Pyramids are the great monuments to the Old Kingdom; the Valley of the Kings on the western bank of the Nile at Thebes houses the tombs of the pharaohs of the New Kingdom. As early as 2000 BC the pyramids were frequently robbed for their riches, so the New Kingdom pharaohs tried to make their burial sites more secure, cutting them deep into the rock face.

We know of the fabulous riches that were buried with these pharaohs because of the tomb of Tutankhamen, the 'boy king' who ruled from 1334 to 1325 BC, dying when he was only seventeen. The archaeologist Howard Carter entered the tomb in 1922 and found it so full of valuables that it took him four years to reach the inner burial chamber: carefully removing the objects one by one took all that time. In the burial chamber he found the coffins of Tutankhamen – the inner coffin enclosed within two larger outer ones. Each of the outer coffins was made of wood overlaid with beaten gold; the inner coffin was solid gold and the mummy itself wore a gold funerary mask weighing over 20 lb. Gilded statues, a magnificent gold throne, gold-handled daggers, ebony carvings and alabaster vases are just some of the riches Carter found.

The discovery was not without its dark side. Carter's patron, Lord Caernarvon, died within weeks of entering the tomb. The cause of death was an infected mosquito bite, a serious wound to a man who was already a semi-invalid. But it was said that at the time of his death the lights went out all over Cairo and his pet dog at home in England suddenly died. Despite the fact that Carter himself lived another fifteen years, dying at the respectable age of 65, the myth of the curse of the pharaohs was born.

The riches of Tutankhamen's tomb captured the imagination of the world as no scientific discovery had ever done before. After her brother's death, Lord Caernarvon's sister Lady Burghclere wrote, 'If it is true that the whole world loves a lover, it is also true that either openly or secretly the world loves Romance. Hence, doubtless, the passionate and far-flung interest aroused by the discovery of Tut-ankh-Amen's tomb, an interest extended to the discoverer, and certainly not lessened by the swift tragedy that waited on his brief hour of triumph. A story that opens like Aladdin's cave and ends like a Greek myth of Nemesis cannot fail to capture the imagination of all men and women who, in this workaday existence, can still be moved by tales of high endeavour and unrelenting doom.' Nor was this fascination short-lived: Tutankhamen's riches toured the world from the late 1960s to the early 1980s and people queued for hours to see them. In San Francisco alone it was estimated that Tut had had eight million visitors.

Tutankhamen is, of course, by no means the only pharaoh commemorated in the Valley of the Kings. The tombs of Ramesses the Great and his father Seti I were entirely hewn out of the rockface, in places alternating limestone and flint. Seti's reign (1291–1278 BC) marked one of the high points of Egyptian art and his tomb contains some of the finest and most extensive of all decorative reliefs. It is also vast, measuring about 300 feet square. Giovanni Belzoni discovered Seti's magnificent alabaster sarcophagus in 1817, and wrote that it 'merits the most particular attention, not having its equal in the world'. The walls of Seti's temple show him and his son

Overleaf. Tutankhamun in his chariot, crushing the Syrian enemy from the north.

making offering to Amun-Ra: only fifty years on, Akhenaten's attempt to suppress this cult in favour of that of the Aten was forgotten.

The nearby site of Deir el-Bahri boasts three of the most magnificent of Middle and New Kingdom temples. It was here that the archaeologist Gaston Maspero discovered a cache of royal mummies (including those of Seti and Ramesses) in 1881.

The oldest of the three temples is that of Mentuhotep I (2060–2010 BC); the least well preserved is that of Hatshepsut's usurped stepson Tuthmosis III (1504–1450 BC). But by far the most famous and most spectacular is the funerary temple of Queen Hatshepsut (1498–1483 BC). A surviving portico shows the two great obelisks ordered by the Queen being brought down river from Aswan. Spacious courtyards and lengthy colonnades show that this was a truly luxurious memorial, while shrines dedicated to Anubis and Hathor remind us of the need to honour the gods, especially in death. The temple was not the first burial place Hatshepsut designed for herself: she had originally intended her tomb to be outside the Valley of the Kings, carved into a remote cliff face. Howard Carter investigated it in 1923 and discovered that it had never been used, although it still contained the sarcophagus intended to hold her mummified body. After this

Opposite. The gold death mask of Tutankhamun which covered the mummy's face within the golden coffin. Tutankhamun was a relatively unimportant pharaoh who died aged seventeen, possibly murdered. It was the discovery of his tomb in 1922 which made him the very symbol of the splendour of Ancient Egypt. His tomb had not altogether escaped the attentions of earlier robbers, but it nevertheless contained a wealth of jewellery and artefacts, the beauty and richness of which captured the world's attention.

discovery, Carter wrote, '...as a king, it was clearly necessary for her to have her tomb in the Valley like all other kings...and the present tomb was abandoned. She would have been better advised to hold to her original plan. In this secret spot her mummy would have had a reasonable chance of avoiding disturbance: in the Valley it had none. A king she would be, and a king's fate she shared.'

Much has been written about the discovery of Tutankhamen's legacy, but surely nothing more evocative than Howard Carter's account of first entering the tomb.

For the moment – an eternity it must have seemed to the others standing by – I was struck dumb with amazement, and when Lord Caernarvon, unable to stand the suspense any longer, inquired anxiously, 'Can you see anything?' it was all I could do to get out the words, 'Yes, wonderful things.'

The gorgeousness of the sight, the sumptuous splendor of it all, made it appear more like the confused magnificence of those counterfeit splendors which are heaped together in the property-room of some modern grand opera than any possible reality surviving from antiquity. Never was anything so dramatic in the whole range of archaeological discovery as this first view vouchsafed us here.

James Breasted, *Some Experiences in the Tomb of Tutenkhamon* (1924)

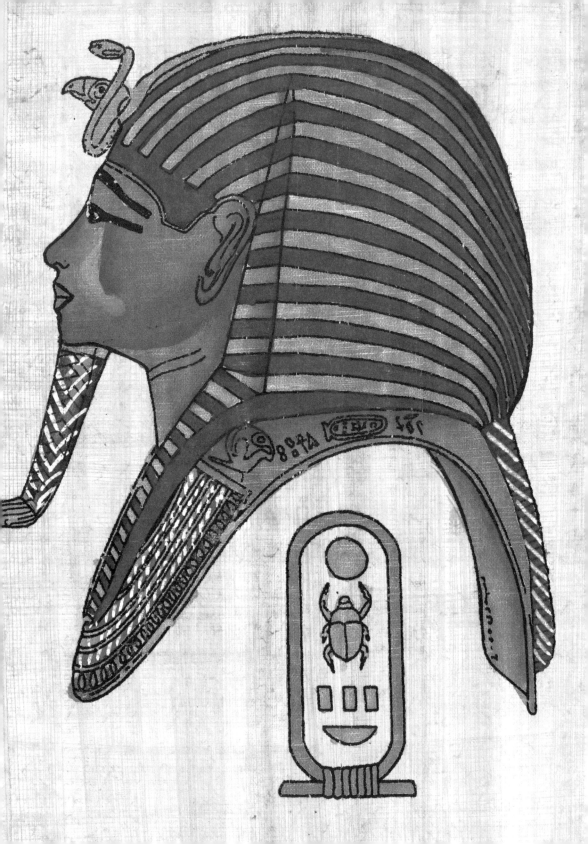

Everywhere there was evidence of the accomplished artist and skilled craftsman, intent on the mysteries of a vanished religion, and the problems of death. Finally we reach the monarch himself, profusely anointed with sacred unguents and covered with numberless amulets and emblems for his betterment, as well as personal ornaments for his glory.

Howard Carter, *The Discovery of the Tomb of Tutankhamen* (vol. 2, 1927)

Painting, in Egypt, at this period, was used merely for ornament; according to all appearance, it was not even a peculiar art: sculpture was emblematic and, so to say, architectural. Architecture, then, was *the* art, by excellence, the art dictated by utility.

Dominique Vivant Denon,
Travels in Upper and Lower Egypt (1803)

The discovery of Tutankhamen's tomb … broke upon a world sated with First World War conferences, with nothing proved and nothing achieved, after a summer journalistically so dull that one English farmer's report of a gooseberry the size of a crab apple achieved the main news pages of the London Metropolitan dailies. It was hardly surprising, therefore, that the Tutankhamen discoveries should have received a volume of world-wide publicity exceeding anything in the history of science.

Charles Breasted, *Pioneer to the Past* (1943)

Four years ago, in the 17th year of the king, my master, we broke into the tomb of King Sebekemsaf and searched it. We opened the outer coffins, then the inner ones. We found the noble mummy of the king dressed as a warrior; it had numerous amulets and gold ornaments around its neck, and its gold headdress was in place. The noble mummy was covered with gold from head to foot, and the inner coffin was inlaid with a great deal of gold and silver, both inside and out, and with all sorts of precious stones. We took the gold from on top of the mummy, as well as the amulets and ornaments from round its neck. We stole all the goods that we could find – gold, silver and bronze objects, that is – and we shared out everything between us, in eight lots.

Confession of a pyramid robber,
c. 1100 BC

I wonder how many of us, born and brought up in the Victorian era, would like to think that in the year, say, 5923, the tomb of Queen Victoria would be invaded by a party of foreigners who robbed it of its contents, took the body of the great Queen from the mausoleum … and exhibited it to all and sundry who might wish to see it? The question arises whether such treatment as we should count unseemly in the case of the great English Queen is not equally unseemly in the case of King Tutankhamen.

Letter to The Times (1923)

I suppose most excavators would confess to a feeling of awe – embarrassment almost – when they break into a chamber closed and sealed by pious hands so many centuries ago ... The very air you breathe, unchanged throughout the centuries, you share with those who laid the mummy to its rest. Time is annihilated by little intimate details such as these, and you feel an intruder.

This is perhaps the first dominant sensation, but others follow thick and fast – the exhilaration of discovery, the fever of suspense, the almost overmastering impulse, born of curiosity, to break down seals and lift the lids of boxes, the thought – pure joy to the investigator – that you are about to add a page to history, or solve some problem of research, the strained expectancy – why not confess it? – of the treasure-seeker.

Howard Carter, *The Discovery of the Tomb of Tutankhamen* (1923)

Without, all was sunshine and splendour; within, all was silence and mystery. A heavy, death-like smell, as of long-imprisoned gases, met us on the threshold. By the half-light that strayed in through the portico, we could see vague outlines of a forest of giant columns rising out of the gloom below and vanishing into the gloom above.

Amelia Edwards,
A Thousand Miles Up the Nile (1877)

Opposite. Tutankhamun with his young wife, Ankhesenpaaten, in a garden.

There is a story about Sir Bruce Ingram, long-time editor of the *Illustrated London News*, who was given a mummy's hand as a paperweight. The wrist was still bound with a copper bracelet set with a scarab. The hieroglyphs on the scarab, translated, proved to be, 'Cursed by he who moves my body. To him shall come fire, water and pestilence.' Several months later the editor's beautiful country house burned to the ground. It was rebuilt and a flood promptly swept through its ground floors. Sir Bruce did not wait for the pestilence. He sent the mummy's hand back to the Valley of Kings. To call this superstition combined with coincidence is the easiest and also the most scientific way out. Nevertheless ...

Henry Field, *The Track of Man* (1955)

In his play *Antony and Cleopatra*, William Shakespeare wrote unforgettably of the Egyptian queen's arrival in Rome:

The barge she sat in, like a burnish'd throne,
Burn'd on the water; the poop was beaten gold,
Purple the sails, and so perfumed, that
The winds were love-sick with them, the oars were silver,
Which to the tune of flutes kept stroke, and made
The water which they beat to follow faster,
As amorous of their strokes. For her own person,
It beggar'd all description; she did lie

Opposite. Cleopatra VII (51–30 BC). This queen, famed for her beauty, fell in love with the Roman general Mark Antony. Their love story, which ended in a joint suicide following her defeat by the Romans, is legendary.

In her pavilion, – cloth-of-gold of tissue, –
O'er-picturing that Venus where we see
The fancy outwork nature; on each side her
Stood pretty-dimpled boys, like smiling Cupids,
With divers-colour'd fans, whose wind did seem
To glow the delicate cheeks which they did cool,
And what they undid did.

The Book of the Dead is a modern name for a
collection of ancient spells which the Egyptians buried
with the deceased to help their passage into the afterlife.
Spell 20 is addressed to Thoth, whose duty it was to
adjudicate on the fate of souls who passed into the next
world:

O Thoth, who protected Osiris against his enemies, entrap
the enemies of this mortal in the presence of the tribunals of
every god and goddess:
In the presence of the great tribunal in Heliopolis on the
night of battle and of felling those who rebelled.
In the presence of the great tribunal in Busiris on that night
of erecting the two djed-pillars.
In the presence of the great tribunal in Letopolis on that
night when the ritual was performed in Letopolis.
In the presence of the great tribunal in Pe and Dep on that
night of confirming the heritage of Horus in respect of the
property of his father Osiris.
In the presence of the great tribunal in the Two Banks on that
night when Isis mourned for her brother Osiris.
In the presence of the great tribunal in Abydos on the
night of the haker-festival and of the numbering of
the dead and the spirits.

In the presence of the great tribunal on the Road of the Dead on that night of making inquiry into him who is nothing. In the presence of the great tribunal in the Great Devastation. In the presence of the great tribunal in Naref. In the presence of the great tribunal in Roset-jau on that night when Horus was vindicated against his enemies. It is good that Horus has become great; the Two Conclaves are pleased, and Osiris rejoices. O Thoth, protect this mortal against his enemies in the tribunal of every god and goddess, and in those tribunals of Osiris which are behind the shrine.

Other spells reflect more earthly concerns. Number 34 hopes to protect the deceased against being bitten by a snake in the realm of the dead:

O cobra, I am the flame which shines on the brows of the Chaos-gods of the Standard of Years. Otherwise said: the Standard of Vegetation. Begone from me, for I am Mafdet!

Spell 36 chases off a beetle:

Begone from me, O crooked lips! For I am Khnum, Lord of Peshnu, who despatches the words of the gods to Re, and I report affairs to their master.

Spell 43 prevents the deceased from being decapitated in the kingdom of the dead:

I am a Great One, the son of a Great One, I am a flame, the son of a flame, to whom was given his head after it had been cut off. The head of Osiris shall not be taken from him, and my head shall not be taken from me. I am knit together, just and young, for I indeed am Osiris, the Lord of Eternity.

The entire journey to Upper Egypt is extremely easy and without the slightest danger of any kind, especially at this season when the heat is far from excessive. Therefore from now on you can change your opinion concerning the Egyptian climate. Mists come up after dark as they do anywhere else. The nights are cold (although the servants, or rather the slaves, sleep in the street, on the ground, outside the house doors), and there are clouds. To listen to some people in France, Egypt is a veritable oven; so it is, but it sometimes cools off. If you would like, darling, to have an inventory of what I wear these days (following the unanimous advice of sensible people here), this is how I dress: flannel body-belt, flannel shirt, flannel drawers, thick trousers, warm vest, thick neck-cloth, with an overcoat besides morning and evening; my head is shaved, and under my red tarboosh I wear two white skull-caps.

Gustave Flaubert, *Letter to his Mother* (1849)

It flows through old hushed Egypt and its sands,
Like some grave mighty thought threading a dream,
And times and things, as in that vision, seem
Keeping along it their eternal stands.

James Leigh Hunt (1784-1859), *The Nile*

A typical family scene. One of the little girls holds a richly jewelled collar. Egyptian goldsmiths produced exquisite work. In spite of the depredations perpetrated by tomb robbers over the centuries – their chief interest was always jewellery, which could easily be melted down and sold for the gold – many dazzling examples of the workmanship have survived. Tutankhamun's tomb was a treasure trove. It was robbed twice in antiquity and only the burial chamber itself was left undisturbed. It must be assumed that most of the stored precious jewellery was taken away, except for seven solid gold rings which were discovered in another chamber, still tied inside a piece of cloth, obviously aban-doned in a hurry. The main hoard of jewellery, now exhibited at the Cairo Museum, was recovered from the king's body. It numbered 170 items.

We waited a good half hour for the sunrise.
The sun was rising just opposite; the whole valley of the
Nile, bathed in mist, seemed to be a still white sea; and
the desert behind us, with its hillocks of sand, another
ocean, deep purple, its waves all petrified. But as the
sun climbed behind the Arabian chain the mist was torn
into great shreds of filmy gauze; the meadows, cut by
canals, were like green lawns with winding borders.
To sum up: three colours – immense green at my feet in
the foreground; the sky pale red – worn vermilion;
behind and to the right, a rolling expanse looking
scorched and iridescent.

Gustave Flaubert, *Travel Notes* (1851)

… beyond the doorway, a strange-looking, stupendous
mass of yellow limestone masonry, long, and low, and
level, and enormously massive … the curved cornice of
a mighty Temple – a Temple neither ruined nor defaced
but buried to the chin in the accumulated rubbish of a
score of centuries.

Amelia Edwards, *A Thousand Miles
Up the Nile* (1877)

The water of the Nile is quite yellow, it carries a good
deal of soil. One might think of it as being weary of all
the countries it has crossed, weary of endlessly murmuring
the same monotonous complaint that it has travelled too
far. If the Niger and the Nile are but one and the same

river, where does this water come from? What has it seen? Like the ocean, this river sends our thoughts back almost incalculable distances; then there is the eternal dream of Cleopatra, and the great memory of the sun, the golden sun of the Pharaohs. As evening fell, the sky turned all red to the right, all pink to the left. The pyramids of Sakkara stood out sharp and grey against the vermilion backdrop of the horizon. An incandescence glowed in all that part of the sky, drenching it with a golden light. On the other bank, to the left, everything was pink; the closer to the earth, the deeper the pink. The pink lifted and paled, becoming yellow, then greenish; then the green itself paled and, almost imperceptibly, through white, became the blue which made the vault above our heads, where there was the final melting of the transition (abrupt) between the two great colours.

Gustave Flaubert, *Travel Notes* (1850)

Perhaps the closing words should go to Dominique Vivant Denon, Napoleon's emissary, whose writings and illustrations almost single-handedly sparked off the passion for Egypt and Egyptology that has continued unabated for nearly two hundred years:

I had primarily intended to have added to my journal some critical digressions on the antiquities, and to have joined to my descriptions discussions on the travellers by whom I have been preceded: I had consulted well-informed persons, in order to add learned notes on the curious objects of which I was to present the image; but, no sooner was I informed that the institute of Caira had effected its voyage in the calm of peace; ...than I gave up the thought of following a plan which others must necessarily execute much better... I have therefore stripped my journal of all the researches on which I had ventured; I have reassumed my uniform of pioneer, and my post in the advanced-guard, where I retain no pretension but that of having planted a few stakes on the road, for the information of those that have to follow, and, were it only by my errors, thus to be serviceable to the editors of the great work: happy, for my own part, if, through my zeal and enthusiasm, I have been enabled to give my reader an idea of a country so important for its own sake and for the ideas it recalls; if I have been enabled truly to present them with its form, its colour, and its peculiar character; if, in fine, as an eye-witness, I have made them acquainted with the details of a grand and extraordinary campaign, itself the principal part of the vast conception of this celebrated expedition: if I have attained this end, it is because I have had the advantage of taking all my drawings and all my descriptions from nature.